Cooking Bouquet

Cooking Bouquet

Feeling at Home in the Kitchen

Arlene Stolley

Cooking Bouquet

Feeling at Home in the Kitchen

© 2006 Arlene Stolley

Written by Arlene Stolley
Illustrated by Eric Cash

Printed in China.

For information, please contact:
Brown Books Publishing Group
16200 North Dallas Parkway, Suite 170
Dallas, Texas 75248
www.brownbooks.com
972-381-0009
A New Era in Publishing

Hardbound ISBN: 1-933285-28-1
LCCN 2006920082
1 2 3 4 5 6 7 8 9 10

www.cookingbouquet.com

Dedication

To the best cook I have ever known—
my grandmother Lorene Cole Phillips.
Her love of food, family gatherings, and sound nutrition
was an inspiration.

Contents

Recipes

Recipes

Recipes

Recipes

Acknowledgments

My heartfelt thanks to:

My husband Scott and daughter Megan for their endless support, savvy critiques, and tireless taste testing.

My sons Clay and Blake for encouraging and supporting me as I made the choice to enter culinary school.

My good friend Marie and her family for dropping everything to come over and pick up dinner from my recipe testing.

My publisher Milli Brown for thinking my idea for this book had great potential.

My editors Deanne Dice and Kathryn Grant for triple checking that my t's were crossed, my i's were dotted, and my commas were in the right place. You two gals are the best.

My Brown Books designer Ted Ruybal for creating such a beautiful book, and Eric Cash for his exceptional watercolors.

My IACP (International Association of Culinary Professionals) colleagues Robin Kline and Linda Behrends for their culinary expertise.

My mentor Chef Michael Scott for his sage advice and for showing me the ins and outs of a professional kitchen.

My high-altitude Colorado baker Marcia Mootz for testing the baked goods high up in the Rocky Mountains.

My Wine-Time advisor Jim Grant of Global Wine Group for expertly pairing the monthly menus with wine selections.

This book would not have been possible without the guidance and mentorship of author Jane Jarrell. I am sincerely grateful to Jane for putting my thoughts and ideas into a cohesive format for my first writing endeavor. Her willingness to taste and test my recipes and her constructive feedback were most appreciated.

Introduction

Cooking is at once child's play and adult joy. And cooking done with care is an act of love.
—Craig Claiborne, *food writer*

He asked, and you said YES! You are officially engaged. Love and life can resemble a whirlwind, especially when you embark on the journey of blending two lives, two homes, and two futures. Welcome to a series of unforgettable firsts you will experience—even before you walk down the aisle. The tabletop selections you make now will grace your home for years to come. Think just a moment about your first candlelit dinner in your new residence, the first time your best friends will drop by for dessert, the first time you will entertain the in-laws. Special events in life usually involve great food, so feeling comfortable in the kitchen is a major ingredient to lifelong culinary ease. Embrace your journey of firsts with a plan in hand.

Registering (for your wedding gifts) for kitchen items you'll need is a superb way to begin setting up your kitchen. Start by selecting the everyday items you will need, from teacups to tool belts. You are beginning to "play house" on a grand scale. Every preschool child playing the game of house has a kitchen stocked with the necessities, even though of the pretend variety. Now you are selecting the real deal. As the kitchen becomes the heart of the home, making proper selections will help ensure a tasty and healthy culinary future.

My kitchen experience goes back twenty-five years. Cooking is my passion, a passion shared with me by my grandmother, who taught me early that food equals love, and that preparing food with and for others shows how much you care. We shared good foods, warm conversation, and generational traditions just by sitting down at the table. My heart's desire is to encourage you—as you blend two families' traditions—to create your own memories as you offer hospitality to those you love. Food traditions are treasured memories established as delicious links to past generations. You will find my culinary style to be approachable, doable, and relaxed. From my own experiences as a seasoned home cook and as a professional chef, I want to help you with the knowledge I have gained through years in the kitchen.

How to Best Use This Book

Cooking Bouquet: Feeling at Home in the Kitchen is more than a cookbook. It is a resource for kitchen setup—from equipment needs to pantry perk-ups. From shopping secrets to perfect poultry, you will find everything you need to create a level of comfort that will make your kitchen preparations a breeze.

What's the first thing that comes to your mind when you think about setting up your new kitchen? Are you delighted with the thought of preparing fabulous meals together, or are you frightened with the overwhelming task of daily meal management? Pour a cup of tea and relax . . . I've done the work for you. Beginning with the basics, what must you have to help run a smooth home kitchen? The answers are in the pages to follow. You will find shopping guidelines and proper ways to prepare the pantry. Once your kitchen is equipped, you will find chapter after chapter of month-to-month menus, simple entertaining ideas, food tips, and more.

The purpose of this book is to offer you confidence as you and your partner create a food history and establish your own traditions. My hope is to help you create a kitchen so special that family and friends cannot wait to visit your home, just to get a whiff of the sensational smells from your stove.

Cookfully yours,

Arlene

Arlene Stolley

Setting the Scene for Success

The items you select as you register for your wedding gifts will be in your home for years. No pressure, right? Pressure is definitely not the key, but planning is. How do you, as a couple, feel most comfortable eating? When you invite guests over, how do you plan to entertain? As you answer these questions together, you will slowly begin to define your "entertaining style," a style that will grow and develop just as you do. So choose wisely, select items of quality, and enjoy lovely things for a lifetime.

Cooking Bouquet is a resource guide for stocking your kitchen with the proper equipment to ensure culinary success . . . whether you are preparing the recipes in this book or those passed down from Mom. In this chapter you will find an itemized list of kitchen equipment to request as you register for gifts. After receiving the gifts, you will find valuable tips for setting up your kitchen and maximizing the space you have. Sprinkled throughout the book is information on how to choose knives, measuring cups, sauté pans, and tabletop necessities. So let's get prepared to enjoy years of good food!

A simple setup for your new kitchen will streamline your meal preparations, give you more confidence, and assist you in preparation using the freshest ingredients. Having the right tools on hand and knowing where they are stored is 90 percent of the job. Good kitchen equipment is an investment that will continue to pay off. Quality pots and pans can be expensive—but with solid warranties and careful handling, cookware can last a lifetime.

Pots, Pans, Utensils

Skillets have sloping sides, and sauté pans have straight sides. Skillets and sauté pans look similar and can be used interchangeably, although a pan with sloping sides is handier for pouring pan juices over sautéed meats. Sizes you will need:

* Nonstick sauté pans

    6-inch sauté pan, also known as an omelet pan

    10-inch pan, with lid (optional)

    12-inch pan, with lid

* Regular skillets made from heavy aluminum or stainless steel.

    10-inch-pan, with lid

    12-inch-pan (3-quart), with lid

    Large stove-top wok (nonstick or regular) for stir-frying.

Perfect Pans

If I had just one pan in my kitchen, it would be a 3-quart skillet with lid. The versatility of this pan is incredible.

Top Pick

* **All-Clad 3-quart stainless-steel skillet.**
    All-Clad has not changed this stainless-steel line since starting thirty years ago, and there is no need to do so. The pan has one of the widest cooking surfaces and can easily fit four chicken breasts. It heats up quickly and maintains an even heat. This pan is heavy-duty without being heavy. Though it carries a hefty price tag, it's a solid investment.

* **KitchenAid 3-quart stainless-steel sauté pan.**
    KitchenAid went into the pots and pans business six years ago, and they're doing a fine job. The center of the pan tends to get hotter than the edges, but you can simply adjust the heat. The flared edge comes in handy when pouring sauce over meats.

- Cast-iron skillet.
  Recommended brand: **Lodge Logic preseasoned**

- Dutch oven. A heavy-bottomed, covered pot with a lid, 4–5 quart.
  Recommended brands: **All-Clad** is an expensive but a solid investment. **Le Creuset** is a pricey but excellent brand.

- Roasting pan. Look for a heavy-bottomed pan large enough to hold a turkey.

- Roasting rack. Preferably nonstick, in a size that fits inside the roasting pan.

- Stove-top grill pan.

- Stove-top griddle skillet, 11-inch.
  Recommended brand: **Calphalon**

- Saucepans, 2- and 3-quart sizes, heavy-bottomed stainless steel with lids.
  Recommended brand: **All-Clad**

- Stockpot, 6–8 quart size, heavy-bottomed, stainless steel, with lid.
  Recommended brand: **Grand Cuisine**

- Nonstick metal loaf pan with insert for meatloaf.
  Recommended brand: **Mirro**

- Glass pan (9x5-inch loaf) is also useful for giving breads a nice, brown crust.
  Recommended brand: **Pyrex**

- Glass baking dishes. A 13x9-inch (3-quart), a 7x11-inch (2-quart), and a 9-inch for pies.
  Recommended brand: **Pyrex**

- 8x8-inch square **Pyrex** pan for baking and small casseroles.

- Two cookie-baking sheets. Look for flat, heavy aluminum.

- Cake pans. 8- or 9-inch round pans, aluminum.
  Recommended brand: **Mirro**

- 13x9-inch rectangular pan, heavy-gauged aluminum (with lid for sheet cakes).
  Recommended brand: **Nordic**

- Bundt cake pan, 12-cup size.
  Recommended brand: **Nordic**

- Cake rack for cooling cakes and cookies. Double-stacking racks save space.

- Casseroles, assorted sizes.
  Recommended brand: **CorningWare**

- Muffin tins. 12- and 6-muffin sizes, aluminum.

- Pie ring to protect the rim of the piecrust from burning.

- 15x10x1-inch baking pan (jelly roll pan). Use for making croutons and roasting vegtables in oven.

- Glass canisters with tightly fitting lids, for flour and sugar storage.

- Mixing bowls, varying sizes. Rubber bottoms keep the bowls stable during mixing.

- Cutting boards. Wooden for fruits and vegetables and polyurethane for meats. (Do not mix the meat cutting boards with the vegetable cutting boards. Using color-coded, polyurethane cutting mats will help you avoid mixing up your boards.)

- Knives in several sizes. An 8- to 10-inch chef's knife, a 3- to 4-inch paring knife, and a bread (serrated) knife.
  Recommended brands: **Wüsthof** and **Henckels**

- ❈ Wooden knife block, or drawer holders to protect blades during storage.

- ❈ Steel. A steel does not sharpen a knife; it is used to straighten the blade between sharpenings. To use a steel, place the knife blade against the steel at a 20-degree angle. Then draw the blade along the entire length of the steel. Repeat several times on both sides of the blade.

- ❈ Colander. A large size for draining pasta and cooked vegetables, and a small size for berries and small amounts of herbs.

- ❈ Sieves or strainers. Small for straining citrus juice, medium round for sifting flour, and large for straining sauces or soups.

- ❈ Corkscrew with a sturdy handle you can grip firmly.

- ❈ Pizza cutter. Look for a large wheel that can cut through extra cheese.
  Recommended brand: **OXO Good Grips**

- ❈ Bottle opener (with a triangular head) to pierce cans of liquid.

- ❈ Instant-read thermometer for meat and poultry.

- ❈ Long-handled meat spatula.

- ❈ Glass measuring cups in 1-, 2-, and 4-cup measurements for liquids.
  Recommended brand: **OXO** (cups have lines set on a diagonal for easier reading)

- ❈ Metal or plastic measuring cups for solid ingredients. Sizes 1, 1/2, 1/3, and 1/4 cup.

- ❈ Measuring spoons. Two sets in graduated sizes— 1 tablespoon, 1 teaspoon, 1/2 teaspoon, 1/4 teaspoon, and 1/8 teaspoon. Narrow, oval-shaped spoons that fit into small spice jars are especially helpful.

- ❈ Silicon-treated pancake turner for use on nonstick surfaces.

- ❈ Metal spatula with 9-inch offset for use on an outdoor grill.

- ❈ Long-handled, spring-loaded tongs for outdoor grill.

- ❈ Metal spatula, straight, for frosting cakes.

- ❈ Oven thermometer to check oven temperatures for accuracy and to use on the outdoor grill.

- ❈ Kitchen scale, manual or electronic.
  Recommended brand: **Salter**

- ❈ Kitchen shears.

- ❈ Pepper grinder.

- ❈ Rolling pin.

- ❈ Rubber spatulas.
  Recommended brand: **Silicon** (they come in great colors)

- ❈ Salt jar for storing salt accessibly.

- ❈ Steamer. Folding basket insert for steaming vegetables in a 2–3 quart sauce pan.

- ❈ Vegetable peeler, swivel-type.

- ❈ Two timers.
  Recommended brands: **Lux** or **OXO Good Grips**

- ❈ Tongs (spring loaded). Keep the 12-inch tongs closed in drawer with rubber bands when storing.

- Wire whisk. A 12-inch and 6-inch mini for incorporating sauces and small amounts of salad dressing. A nonstick whisk for nonstick cookware.

- Wooden spoons, assorted sizes.

- Broiler pan.

- Nonstick cooking spoon (silicon treated).

- Cooking spoons in varying sizes, plain and slotted.

- Ladle for soups and sauces.

- Potato masher.

- Meat mallet.

- Cheese slicer.

- Box-type grater.

- Small grater for zesting citrus rind and grating hard cheeses. Recommended brand: *Microplane*

- Pastry brush.

- Melon baller.

- Kitchen ruler. Stainless steel or plastic.

- Jar opener. A simple rubber disk.

- Meat carving fork and knife, large and heavy.

- Handheld can opener. Recommended brand: *OXO Good Grips*

- Small custard cups (6 ounce).

- Decorative salad-serving tongs.

- Parchment paper for lining cookie sheets and baking pans. (See cook's note, page 141.)

- Foil.

- Paper muffin cups.

- Plastic wrap.

- Self-sealing plastic storage bags, regular and heavy-duty freezer.

- Mortar and pestle.

- Potholders.

- Trivets.

Electric Appliances

- Slow Cooker. A 3-quart is perfect for two. Recommended brand: *Rival*

- Food processor with small bowl insert. Recommended brand: *KitchenAid*

- Stand mixer. Recommended brand: *KitchenAid*

- Blender. Recommended brand: *Oster*

- Toaster. Recommended brand: *Krups Sensotoaster*

- Handheld electric mixer. Recommended brand: *Black and Decker*

- Panini grill. Recommended brand: *George Foreman*

- Small electric griddle.

Design and Dine

A good kitchen setup is the first step toward cooking success. Why? When you have a place for everything, and everything is in its place, your preparation time is reduced because you do not waste precious time hunting for what you need. Customizing your kitchen layout from the beginning will add immensely to your cooking readiness.

Fluff and Stuff

The most common issue in kitchen readiness is having too much stuff that you don't use in the kitchen and not enough room to store what you really need. Try these tips for being storage savvy:

❀ If you have an island, install a hanging rack above the island and hang the utensils you use most. Just reaching up and grabbing what you need is a real time-saver.

❀ Place a tall, round container on top of the counter nearest the stove, for long-handled spoons, spatulas, whisks, and such that you use every time you cook.

❀ Store silverware, plates, bowls, and glasses near the sink. Whether you are unloading a dishwasher or washing dishes in the sink, storing dishes nearby is convenient.

❀ Keep pots and pans near the stove.

❀ Place baking dishes, casseroles, and mixing bowls near the countertop used most frequently to assemble ingredients.

❀ Counter space is of primary importance in every phase of cooking. Even during step one (shopping) in meal preparation, you need to have space to put the bags down when you get home from the store.

❀ In the lower areas of your kitchen, have drawers instead of cabinets. It is easier to see into a drawer than to get down on your hands and knees to unload the cabinet just to find what you need.

❀ A trash drawer is a great feature, too. This is a tall drawer that can house a large trash container. Any mess you have on the counter can be wiped off directly into the drawer rather than collected and thrown away in some other area of the kitchen.

Kitchen Organization Capers

The kitchen is an area of your home that gets used more often than most other areas, so it stands to reason that if your kitchen starts off organized and simple to use, your life will feel easier. Monica Ricci, a professional organizer of the Catalyst Organizing Solutions, offers ten easy steps to organize your kitchen and make your family life flow more smoothly when it comes to meal preparation.

1. When combining two households, pull everything out of each cabinet and go through it. Discard or donate those things that are not frequently used, duplicate items, broken items, or things you forgot you had. Do this with each cabinet and drawer, setting up separate areas on the floor for each group. Be ruthless. Most kitchens are short on storage space, so the goal is to have only things you love and use.

2. After your cabinets are empty, consider what is best for you in terms of how to group items. Sort all your baking items, and pile them together. Sort your cooking items, and pile them together. Group together the dishes you eat from most often, glassware, holiday, or other seasonal items that get used only once or twice a year, as well as those special entertaining or serving pieces that are used occasionally.

3. Now that you have the groups laid out on the floor, decide where each item should be stored. Cooking and baking pieces should be kept close to where you do food preparation. Utensils should be in the drawer nearest to the prep area as well. Glassware might be best near the sink or refrigerator. Make a coffee or tea station that includes sugar, mugs, and filters, and place it near the water source if possible. This way you avoid going back and forth across the kitchen for the things you need just to make your morning beverage.

4. Containerize your cabinets. Group together things like packets of sauce mixes, small packets of seasoning, hot cereal packets, and hot cocoa envelopes, and put them into small plastic containers or baskets to avoid them being scattered all over the cabinet. Use clear, plastic shoe boxes to store food that is in tiny boxes, such as gelatin or pudding mix.

5. Discard containers without lids, and store the remaining plastic containers either with the lids on them or store the lids in another larger container so they all stay together. Do the same with the lids for your pots and pans. A large, clear plastic box will keep lids together nicely on their sides. Another option is to store lids on their sides on a wire rack in the cabinet.

6. Make use of vertical space. Place hooks underneath cabinets to hold mugs above the countertop, or hang a stemware rack in the same spot for wine glasses. This will free up a lot of cabinet space. You can also hang adhesive hooks on the inside of cabinet doors or pantry doors to hold tools such as measuring

cups, oven mitts, and other kitchen gadgets. Consider using wall space or a ceiling rack to hang pots and pans. Keep in mind that any space you can use to hang something will free up flat space inside a cabinet.

7   Use a lazy Susan (a rotating tray) to hold things such as oils, vinegars, spices, and other cooking ingredients. You can use a few lazy Susans in your refrigerator (even one for beverages!) so nothing ever hides in the back to spoil or freeze. Try an additional lazy Susan for leftovers or small jars of pickles, olives, or other small food items.

8   Use drawer dividers for cooking utensil drawers. Drawer dividers will allow you to assign an individual spot for each thing, and you'll be able to find the utensils more easily when you need them.

9   Get a magnetic sorter box to hang on the side of the refrigerator. Store coupons, takeout menus, a notepad and pen, or other papers that tend to accumulate on the countertops. Each type of item should have its own section in the sorter.

10   Keep trash bags near the trash can, and throw a stack of loose bags into the bottom of the can. That way, when you remove a full bag, there is already another waiting to be used. If you put your trash out at the curb one night a week, use that time to clean out your refrigerator each week, too. See what food needs to be pitched and immediately throw it out. Your refrigerator will house only current items and will be less cluttered—and it only takes a few minutes.

Your personal work style will determine where you store and use the items in your kitchen, but the goal is to get the room and its contents to serve your needs as smoothly and efficiently as possible. If you invest the time and energy into decluttering and organizing your kitchen, it is an investment that will pay off in happiness for years to come.

Toast of the Town

Before purchasing any toasting equipment, consider your counter space and your toasting needs. Although modern toasters sport a galaxy of features, for me it all comes down to:

❈ Even toasting

❈ Color control

❈ Bread widths accepted

❈ Easy-to-clean interior

Many toasters currently on the market have high prices without offering extensive options. So after doing a lot of research, I settled on a *Krups Sensotoaster Deluxe*. It grasps the bread, has nearly foot-long slots, and browns perfectly. Plus, it costs less than fifty dollars.

A Cut Above

There is a different knife for every cutting task: filleting, boning, slicing, dicing, and carving. Investing in good knives will simplify your preparation process for years. Wash and dry knives by hand, not in the dishwasher where they could bang around and become nicked. Store them in a wooden block, wall rack, or in a drawer with the blades separated and protected. Use a sharpening stone called a whetstone—or better yet, have your knives professionally sharpened two or three times a year.

* **Paring knife.** Used for peeling and slicing fruits and vegetables, sculpting garnishes, or chopping small amounts of herbs.

* **Utility knife.** Bigger than a paring knife, the utility knife handles similar tasks and is also handy for carving poultry.

* **Chef's knife.** The large, relatively heavy blade gives good leverage for chopping, slicing, dicing, and mincing. It is often used with a rocking motion.

* **Carving knife.** The blade is long but a bit thinner than a chef's knife. Use it to cut roast beef and whole roasted poultry.

* **Boning knife.** The narrow, tapered blade offers the best maneuverability when cutting up poultry and removing bones.

* **Serrated knife.** Use it for foods—such as bread or angel food cake—that might be compressed by a regular knife blade. The best technique is a back and forth sawing motion with light downward pressure.

* **Steak knives.** A set of six comes in handy.

Measuring Up

Dry Measuring Cups

These cups are indispensable for measuring dry ingredients, especially when baking cookies and cakes. Dry measuring cups are usually made of metal, but you can also find plastic and ceramic cups. They typically come in sets of four sizes: 1 cup, 1/2 cup, 1/3 cup, and 1/4 cup. Other volumes ranging from 1/8 cup to 1 ½ cups are also available. Be sure the cups sit flat, and that they have spouts for easier pouring. For baking recipes, always measure dry ingredients—such as flour, sugar, cornmeal, and nuts—with these cups. They are also good for measuring rice, cheese, vegetables, and herbs. Do not use them to measure liquids.

Liquid Measuring Cups

Liquid measuring cups are made of tempered glass and range in size from 1 to 4 cups. To use, simply pour in the liquid, and read the measurement at eye level.

The Pot Patrol

When you are buying pots and pans, hold them while you are in the store, and decide if you like the way the handle feels. Imagine lifting a large potfull of liquid. Also make sure they are oven safe. Make sure at least some of your pots have tight-fitting lids. Stay away from bargain-basement brands. They dent and warp easily.

You don't have to be a food scientist to understand the materials used for cookware, and a brief overview will help you select wisely.

❋ Aluminum heats quickly and evenly, but it is not the best choice for long, slow cooking. It's great to boil water for pasta and blanching. Aluminum reacts with acidic ingredients, such as tomatoes and vinegar, and imparts a metallic taste.

❋ Anodized aluminum and aluminized steel are alloys that often have a stainless-steel core and are used to make a host of quality pots and pans. You won't go wrong with these.

❋ Cast iron is an old-fashioned material that nonetheless can't be beat for retaining consistent heat, even at very high temperatures. Do not use cast iron with acidic foods.

❋ Glass holds heat well but does not conduct heat quite as efficiently as metal. Tempered glass works on stove tops and in ovens and produces beautiful brown crusts on baked foods.

❋ Nonstick cookware is very effective these days. Use good, heavy, nonstick skillets and saucepans.

Seasoning the Skillet

A cast-iron skillet is exceptional for browning meats. Cast-iron skillets need extra care. Many brands require "seasoning" when purchased and periodic care to maintain seasoning. To season a new cast-iron skillet, start by preheating the oven to 350 degrees (all temperatures in this book will be given in Fahrenheit). Wash, rinse, and dry the skillet. Brush all over with melted shortening. Place upside down in oven for 1 hour. Turn the oven off and let cool. To cleanse after use, scrub with a paste of kosher salt and hot water. To dry, place for 10 minutes in an oven heated to 200 degrees. Avoid detergents. Do not place in the dishwasher. Season as needed if rust or discoloration occurs. You may also find a skillet that is preseasoned, saving you this initial step.

Whisks

You may be surprised at how many common tasks you can accomplish in the kitchen with these classic tools.

What they're good for:

Handheld whisks are designed to blend ingredients without lumping and to incorporate air into liquids. Whisks are ideal for making dressings, blending sauces, beating eggs, and whipping heavy cream. They're also good for whisking together dry ingredients when baking. You can even use them to break up ground meat during cooking.

What to look for:

Whisks should be sturdy, durable, and comfortable feeling in your hand. Choose a whisk with the most wires (it will work the fastest). Make sure the wires are embedded securely in the handle. Most whisks are made of rustproof stainless steel and have nylon-coated wires that are safe to use on nonstick surfaces. Longer whisks can reach into pots and pans; shorter whisks are useful for mixing in bowls.

A Space of Grace

If you have a small kitchen and limited counter space, you can still cook and even entertain. Here's how:

❊ Minimize. Keep only what you use. Less clutter equals less frustration. Store items you do not use often. For easy recall, make a list of these items and their locations, and keep the list on the back of the cabinet or in a utility drawer.

❊ Choose compact appliances. Small appliances will offer you more counter space. Choose mini processors, handheld mixers, and a smaller-scale coffee pot.

❊ Keep cookbooks in bookcases. Photocopy favorite recipes and place in a photo album labeled "Recipes."

❊ Going up? If you do not have shelving in your kitchen, add some. Consider placing a peg-board on your wall to hang utensils, strainers, pots, and pans.

❊ Clean as you go. Fill your sink or a large bowl with warm soapy water. Place your dirty utensils in the water as you finish using them. Have a "trash" bowl at your work area for vegetable peelings, paper towels, and other items used as you cook.

❊ Create decorative counters. Expand your counter space by hunting for horizontal surfaces. Set up an ironing board or open a drawer and top it with a cookie sheet to have an additional work surface. Use the top of the refrigerator to hold equipment you are not using. Drape kitchen equipment with colorful, fun-print cloth napkins, and put decorative kitchen accessories around. Ta-da! Instant kitchen display.

❊ Organize. Use a magazine holder to organize foil, wax paper, and plastic wrap. This will free up much-needed drawer space.

Tabletop Tips

Setting your dining table can be an art. If you have the talent and desire, a mix-and-match philosophy can be quite effective. Mixing sterling with unmatched crockery can be visually stimulating. Traditional lace and linen will always be a beautiful covering for your table, but did you know that in early America, antique quilts were used as tablecloths? With all the table-setting products available, knowing what to buy will help you avoid expensive errors.

❋ Starting with the most costly flatware, sterling silver has beauty, structure, and value. By law, if it is called sterling, it is required to contain 92.5 percent silver. No wonder burglars steal the sterling! The price depends on how heavy the pattern is and how intricate the design. Sterling is the stuff of which heirlooms are made. Age and use only enrich its beauty.

❋ Sterling II is a new-generation silver—sterling coupled with stainless steel. Sterling II costs about half as much as sterling.

❋ Silver plate is an outer layer of pure silver, electroplated over nickel and silver. The better quality silver plate has a double layer of silver over the most vulnerable areas of the flatware. You get the beauty of sterling at a much lower cost.

❋ Gold electroplate employs the same technique as silver electroplate, but 24-karat gold is used instead of silver. Some sterling or silver-plate flatware is accented or edged with gold electroplate. Lofty price, but a great look.

❋ Stainless used to be standard for informal dining, but lately it's been fancied up enough to be used in formal settings. You might remember it as stainless steel. It is made up of steel, chrome, and nickel. A pattern carrying a number 18/8 means the flatware is made of 18 percent chrome and 8 percent nickel, with a balance of steel. High chrome and nickel are desirable as they increase the pieces' resistance to wear and washing. Stainless is affordably priced.

* Pewter has improved since colonial days. Now pewter is lead free, won't tarnish, and is dish-washer safe. Be sure to check the label to ensure that the pewter is safe to use with food.

* Like flatware, dishes have a pecking order of their own, with the pinnacle being fine china. China is a delicate-looking, translucent piece that glows when you hold it to the light and "sings" when you tap it. You have porcelain and bone china to choose from. Though both appear fragile, they are fired at very high temperatures that leave them strong and chip resistant. Nevertheless, I don't recommend playing catch with them.

* Vitreous or semi-vitreous (glass-like) china looks and feels like porcelain or bone china, but it is less expensive.

* Stoneware, a notch lower in the pricing hierarchy, is also fired at high temperatures but is decidedly heavier, more durable, and ideal for tough, everyday usage.

* Earthenware is also heavy, but tends to chip more easily than china and stoneware. If your house-hold has a history of butterfingers in the kitchen, stoneware is your answer. It's harder to break.

* Stemware is next on the list. Crystal is high-quality, high-priced glass to which a certain amount of lead has been added, resulting in a sparkle and a "ring" when tapped. The more lead, the finer the china.

* European stemware may contain 24–35 percent lead, while American stemware might range from 10–24 percent. Lead softens the glass, which allows for finer, more delicate decorating on the glass. The artisan creates hand-blown glass, giving each piece its individuality. Machine-blown glass is beautiful but not as expensive.

* Table covers, affectionately known as linens, are often a blend of man-made linen look-alikes. They are ready-to-wear, drip dry, no iron—the American way of life. So now that you have the easy-care tablecloths, what is the proper size "linen" for your table? A formal cloth drops 16–24 inches all around. The informal look requires 10–14 inches.

Savvy Shopping

So you have selected your kitchen companions, also known as the necessary pots and pans, equipment, and tools. The next step is reviewing the best ways to shop for the foods you will prepare. Savvy shopping is key to making your menus sizzle. Do you realize shoppers spend $1 for every minute over thirty that they stay in the supermarket? It's true. Becoming a smart shopper matters not only to your waistline but also to your pocketbook.

Stocking your kitchen starts with shopping, and shopping starts with a list. Keep a master shopping list out and available at all times for "at-a-glance" updates on what you might need next. Every time you notice that you are running low on anything, write it on the list. Never go to the supermarket without a shopping list. Not only does having a list save you time, it saves you money. You are much less likely to be seduced into buying all those heavily advertised, cleverly displayed, and usually overpriced food items if you know what and when you need an item.

Learning to be a wise shopper will make you a successful shopper. What is the secret to being a super shopper?

❁ Determine the day of the week that is least hectic for you.

❁ Decide what time during the day you can work in one hour of shopping.

❁ Plan three or four meals in advance, and use the most perishable items first.

❁ Don't forget the list. It saves time and money, and offers ease in recipe preparation.

❁ Shop at the same supermarket on a regular basis. This helps you to know the store's layout and offered specials.

❁ When making your shopping list, divide it into categories that reflect the layout of your supermarket.

❁ Don't shop when you are hungry. You will buy too much.

❁ Keep a week-to-week price list until you become familiar with regular food prices. Then you will be able to decide which specials are good deals.

❁ Always start shopping in the middle of the supermarket where all the dry pantry items are located. You don't want to pile heavy cans, bottles, and boxes on your fresh fruits and vegetables. Plus, you don't want to have fresh fish, poultry, meat, and dairy products off refrigeration for any longer than necessary—nor do you want ice cream melting.

❁ Buy fresh fruits in season when the abundance is greatest and the price is the lowest. Eat asparagus in the spring, nectarines in the summer, apples in the fall, and oranges in the winter.

* Bigger is not always better—even when it is cheaper. When planning meals for two people, don't buy large economy-sized boxes of crackers or breakfast cereal because they will often become stale and have to be thrown away.

* Obvious but critical—always check the expiration date on packaged goods of all types, so you don't waste money on outdated products.

* If your supermarket has a butcher, get on friendly terms with him or her. You might be surprised how happy your butcher is to answer questions you may have about various cuts of meat.

* Clear some space by cleaning out the fridge before shopping each week. Make room for new groceries.

* Take advantage of unadvertised store specials.

* High-profit items are placed at eye level. Stretch and bend for bargains.

* Use coupons for items you repeatedly buy.

* Never buy a canned product that has a dent in the can. The inside of the can could be cracked, which creates a haven for bacteria to grow.

* Check the registry tape. Scanners can make mistakes.

* Do some prep work as you unpack your groceries. Wash and dry some produce, such as lettuce and herbs, and store it in the refrigerator's vegetable drawer. This will make cooking on busy weeknights faster. (Don't do this with berries; moisture may cause them to spoil.)

* Try "alternative shopping." Explore the local farmers' market and health- or natural-foods market.

A Fresh Approach

Different dating systems are used to tell the consumer about a product's freshness or shelf life. Diane Werner, a registered dietician, shares her knowledge of expiration dates below.

There are two types of date-related information on foods. Closed or coded dating appears on shelf-stable products such as canned goods and boxed items. Used to identify batch runs, closed dates are generally not very useful to the consumer.

Open dating, however, is the system used by shoppers from coast to coast. These dates appear on perishables.

There are three basic types of open dates.

❀ "Best-if-used-by" date: for the best flavor or quality, use the product before this date. It is not a safety date, however.

❀ "Use-by" date: this is the last date recommended for the use of the product while it's at peak quality. It is best to use the product by this date.

❀ "Sell-by" date: this date indicates when stores should remove the product from display. Always purchase food before its sell-by date expires. How long the food is safe to eat after this date depends on the item itself.

The Logic of Labels

Even though labels giving all of the nutrition facts are now mandatory, there are still label-reading pitfalls that can be overcome just by knowing what they are.

❀ All nutritional information is given for one serving, not the entire package, so the first thing to look for is the number of servings per container. Often buyers assume very small packages of high-calorie items contain only a single serving. But rather than eating only 100 calories worth of spread or dip, for example, they may be consuming a whopping 400 calories of it.

❀ If you want to compute the percentage of calories from fat, a simplified way is to multiply the number of fat grams by 10. There are actually 9 calories in a gram of fat, but it's easier to round it off to 10. Then divide this number by the total number of calories. The answer is the percentage of fat calories.

❀ When you're looking for whole-grain bread, make sure that the first ingredient listed is, in fact, whole grain flour. If it is simply wheat flour, it's not what you want to buy.

❀ To avoid products filled with preservatives, don't buy anything with too many words that you can't pronounce on the label.

❀ When it comes to choosing between brand names and generics, there is no hard and fast rule. (By generic brands, I mean those—with store labels—usually less expensive than their nationally advertised counterparts.) The only real test is to buy both and compare the quality. It simply comes down to cost versus quality.

Proper Food Handling

Washing Hands

Proper food handling is essential. The main concerns are cleanliness, preventing cross contamination, and keeping foods at safe temperatures. Gathering a little knowledge and practicing some safe habits will save you a lot of misery.

Wash hands thoroughly with hot soapy water for a minimum of twenty seconds. Remember to lather up to the elbow. Pay special attention to nails and fingertips. Hand washing is one of the easiest and most crucial steps in food safety. Rings and bracelets can harbor germs, so either remove them or wash them carefully. It is important to wash hands in the following situations:

- Before the start of food preparation.

- Between handling different food items, such as raw meat, poultry, fish, and vegetables (and don't forget to wipe off the faucet).

- After touching a pet.

- After handling garbage.

- After touching your face or hair.

Tasting Food

- When tasting food while cooking, always use a separate tasting spoon, and get a new one each time. Do not double dip, and do not eat off the utensil you are using to stir.

- Do not use your fingers to taste. It is not sanitary and you may get a burn if the food is very hot.

- Always handle a tasting spoon by the stem, never by the scoop.

Handling Injuries

❋ If you get cut, quickly apply pressure. Clean and bandage the cut, then clean the knife and cutting board accordingly.

❋ Always wear latex or rubber gloves when you have bandages on your hands. Change the bandage often.

Preventing Cross Contamination

Bacteria from raw meats can be spread to other foods, utensils, or surfaces, and can cause cross contamination, the primary cause of which is preparing raw meats alongside ready-to-eat foods. It's important to know how to cook safely in order to prevent possible problems with cross contamination and food-borne illnesses.

❋ Always separate raw meats from produce and ready-to-eat foods.

❋ At the store, have the cashier bag raw meats separately.

❋ At home, always store raw meats on the bottom shelf of the refrigerator so meat juices won't drip on other foods.

Kitchen Counters

❋ Wash well with hot soapy water, and then use a disinfectant.

❋ Do not let pets walk on work surfaces, and don't sit on work surfaces.

❋ Whenever you have finished working with one food, clean the counters well before introducing a new food.

Cutting Boards

❋ It is a good idea to have separate cutting boards—one for meat, fish, and poultry, and one for produce.

- Sanitize wooden cutting boards by rubbing with distilled grain vinegar, then air drying.

- Cutting boards, especially wooden ones, should be visually checked to ensure that food is not getting imbedded in cracks or crevices.

- Throw out cutting boards when they get excessively worn or when hard-to-clean cracks appear.

- Wash plastic cutting boards with hot soapy water after each use, then sanitize the board with a bleach solution (add 1 tablespoon of bleach to 1 quart cool water, and discard solution daily).

- Plastic cutting boards may be put in the dishwasher, in which case the bleach solution would not be necessary.

Kitchen Dishcloths, Sponges, and Aprons

- Repeatedly using the same cloth or sponge to wipe counters spreads germs. Remember to wash towels daily in the washing machine, and to put sponges in the dishwasher often. Or better yet, don't get in the habit of using sponges.

- Avoid wiping your hands on your apron because you may pick up bacteria from the last time you wiped your hands.

- When handling dishes, allow them to air dry. Don't use cloth towels to dry them as this will spread germs.

Utensils and Serving Pieces for Cooked and Raw Food

- If you take raw meat, poultry, or fish to the outdoor grill, have a new container to put the food on after it is cooked.

- Wash or replace cutlery and utensils that were used while product was raw.

- If your meat, poultry, or seafood was in a marinade, bring the marinade to a boil for at least three minutes before using as a sauce.

Uncooked Foods

❊ Wash lettuce well (even prewashed) by soaking it in a bowl of cool, fresh water.

❊ Clean berries and other fruits with running water. The friction of the water will brush off dirt.

❊ It is important to wash melons and other large fruits and vegetables that are not going to be cooked. Remember, they came from a farm, grew in dirt, and have been handled by numerous people. If you cut an unwashed melon, the knife will push bacteria from the surface to the inside of the melon.

❊ To prevent cross contamination, always wash foods in a bowl, not in a water-filled sink.

❊ If you wash raw chicken, meat, or fish, be sure to wash out the sink well to prevent cross contamination.

❊ When using a food thermometer, always wash it between uses.

❊ Frequent hand washing is crucial in preventing cross contamination.

Temperatures

The food safety and inspection service of the USDA recommends the following safe internal temperatures for serving various meats. These temperature suggestions will be your guide as you cook various meat recipes in the chapters ahead.

Fresh Beef, Veal, Lamb:	
Medium Rare	130 degrees
Medium	145 degrees
Fresh Pork:	
Whole Roast	160 degrees
Pork Tenderloin	150 degrees
Poultry:	
Breast	170 degrees

Stranger Danger

Bacteria grow rapidly between the temperatures of 41 and 135 degrees. This temperature range is known as the "Danger Zone." Pathogenic bacteria thrive in the "Danger Zone." To properly store, hold, and cook foods, it is imperative to minimize the amount of time foods spend at these temperatures. Certain strains can double in number every twenty minutes. These bacteria cause food-borne illnesses but do not affect taste, smell, or appearance.

* Any foods that have been in the temperature range of 41–135 degrees for two hours or more should be discarded; they might taste all right, but could cause severe food-borne illness.

* Don't marinate food at room temperature for longer than one hour.

Quickly Cooling Soups, Stocks, and Hot Liquids

When making a large batch of soup or stew, it can often take a long time to cool. Since foods should not be in the "Danger Zone" for more than two hours, here are some pointers to cool foods quickly.

* Liquids are best cooled in metal containers. Plastic insulates heat and cools more slowly. Use shallow containers for soups and stews.

* Set container in an ice-water bath that reaches the same level as the liquid in the container.

* Stir ingredients occasionally to accelerate cooling.

* Large cuts of meat, like a roast, should be cut into smaller pieces.

Storage Instructions and "Use-by" Dates

Pay attention to storage instructions, such as "refrigerate after opening," and to dates on containers. If items have been stored improperly, it is safest to discard them instead of risking illness.

Mise En Place

This French cooking term should be a part of every home cook's vocabulary—not to impress, but because it holds the secret to the most fundamental cooking tip of all: "everything in its place." By following the principles of *mise en place* as you progress through a recipe, you will become a quicker, more efficient, and cleaner cook.

Recipes are like road maps. The first time you follow one, you need a little more time to get to the destination. Once you are familiar with the route, it is easier to go faster. Eventually, you may not even need the map.

To understand a recipe, read through it entirely first. Roughly plan out the sequence of steps to help determine timing, a critical factor when coordinating several dishes to be served at the same time. If you are preparing more than one recipe, an initial read-through of each allows you to make judgments about timing or about doing similar tasks at the same time. Reading ahead also warns you about recipes within recipes, such as precooking an ingredient (roasting garlic for instance) or preparing a sauce. If you plan to multiply or divide the recipe, make sure to read it all the way through first so that you can make necessary adjustments.

Assemble all the ingredients in front of you before you start cooking. Nothing frazzles a cook more than having to look for an ingredient in the middle of cooking, especially if you find that you're fresh out.

Measure and prepare all ingredients and equipment ahead of time. This means doing any washing, trimming, chopping, slicing, sifting, melting, toasting, or chilling called for in the recipe. Also, grease baking pans, if necessary, and prepare other equipment as required. Whenever possible, combine ingredients that will be going into the pot at the same time. Everything you need should be measured, prepped, and ready to go before you actually start cooking. This is especially helpful when stir-frying or sautéing because the actual cooking time is very short.

To organize ingredients, have small plates and bowls on hand to hold chopped ingredients. Disposable paper cups and bowls are perfect for this task. If you are using them for dry ingredients, they can be wiped out and used again.

To save prep time, accomplish like tasks together. Assemble all of your produce first, then wash it, dry it, and chop it at the same time—rather than preparing the carrots, then the celery, then the beans. This will simplify your movement around the kitchen and keep all your activity in one place at a time, saving total prep time.

To save cleanup time, clean as you go. A tidy workspace goes a long way toward helping you cook more efficiently—and safely.

The Prepared Pantry

Preparing your pantry is paramount. Why? You will be ready to cook at a moment's notice. The key is planning from the get-go. Once you have your plan, work your plan as long as you both shall live. Think about it. Nothing can ruin a meal faster than discovering at the last minute that you're missing a key ingredient. So let's look at the best ways to stock your pantry.

Begin by stocking the basics—common staples used frequently in everyday cooking and baking. Add to these ingredients as your tastes and recipe repertoire develop. Discovering special condiments, favorite packaged side dishes, and extraordinary seasonings is part of the adventure of shopping and trying new recipes.

Another terrific time tip involves having ingredients on hand so you can prepare meals quickly. Circumstances—like unexpected company, a hard day at the office for you both, or needing to get out the door quickly for an evening of fun—make fast meal prep a priority. Impromptu dishes, while still being quite delicious, can be put together on short notice when your time is limited.

Quality Counts

A dish can be no better than the quality of the ingredients it contains. Buy good quality products—all brands are not the same! Often, the incremental cost of purchasing a better brand is nominal when you consider the quantity used and its impact on flavor. Test generic products carefully; some are comparable to "name" brands, and others are poor substitutes.

For purposes of providing a basic list, I've provided suggestions for certain product brands that tested well in the recipes included in this book. The list is by no means inclusive because every day, new and better products become available. Experiment to find products that appeal to your taste and fit your budget.

Setting Up Your Pantry

Think of your pantry as three separate categories:

❀ **The dry pantry.** Items you will keep in cupboards or closets.

❀ **The refrigerator.** Items that must stay chilled.

❀ **The freezer.** Items that must stay frozen.

Let's take a look at how to set up all three for optimum kitchen preparation.

The Dry Pantry

Dry pantry items are "shelf stable"—they need no refrigeration or do not need to be refrigerated until opened. Think cereal, crackers, chips, and packaged snacks.

Tips for Setting Up Your Dry Pantry

* Start with clean, dry shelving, covered with a washable plastic liner.

* Remember, most items should be kept in a cool, dark place to retain maximum freshness. Herbs, spices, and cooking oils are particularly heat-sensitive and should not be stored near appliances that generate heat, such as the oven or range top.

* Maximize storage with specialized products, such as turntables, tiered shelves, baskets, and door racks. You can find these in stores and catalogs specializing in containers.

* Use airtight canisters or jars to store products that are susceptible to damage from moisture and pests. Red spices are particularly attractive to pests and are best kept under refrigeration. Other products particularly at risk include flour, barley, and dried beans. If you have the space, you may want to store vulnerable items in airtight packaging in the freezer.

* Many products expire over time. With a permanent pen, write the date of purchase on the back of spices. Rotate all items so that the oldest are used first. Periodically (every nine months or so) throw away products that are out of date. Spices, in particular, lose potency in about nine months to a year and should be replaced.

* Reserve a small amount of space, perhaps in a basket or tray, to collect those items purchased for recipes you'll be making in the next few days.

* Above all, don't overstock and overcrowd your pantry. It is useless to store items you can't find when you need them. Buy small quantities of items you will use only in limited amounts, especially those that expire, such as spices. Keep the space neatly organized. Group items by category—such as baking supplies, spices, canned goods, and condiments—placing those used most often in the most accessible space.

Basics for the Dry Pantry

❀ All-purpose flour

❀ Almond extract

❀ Baking powder
Recommended brand: *Rumford*

❀ Baking soda

❀ Barbecue sauce

❀ Biscuit mix
Recommended brand: *Bisquick*

❀ Bread crumbs, panko (Japanese)
and Italian

❀ Capers, brined

❀ Club Soda, petite bottles

❀ Cornmeal

❀ Cornstarch

❀ Espresso powder or instant coffee
(used in baking desserts)

❀ Hot pepper sauce
Recommended brand: *Tabasco*

❀ Ketchup

❀ Mayonnaise

❀ Mustards, regular, Dijon, and
spicy brown

❀ Nonfat instant milk

❀ Oatmeal

❀ Olives, black, Spanish, and kalamata

❀ Peanut butter

❀ Powdered buttermilk

❀ Salad dressings
Recommended brands: *Paul
Newman* and *Brianna's*

❀ Soy sauce
Recommended brand: *Tamari*

❀ Teriyaki sauce

❀ Unsweetened baking cocoa

❀ Vanilla extract
Recommended brand: Pure product
from Madagascar

❀ Worcestershire sauce

Pantry Wines to Be Used in Cooking

Never use a product labeled "cooking wine," as this type of wine tends to be loaded with sodium and has a vastly inferior taste. For cooking, purchase wines that you would enjoy drinking. Once opened, wine does not keep well. Consider shopping for wines in small containers. Brands such as *Cavita Collection* are available in four packs of 187ml bottles, which equates to about 3/4 cup. Leftover red wine can be frozen successfully for future use in cooking; white wine does not freeze well.

Suggested varieties:

Sherry	Medium-dry sherry (can be kept unrefrigerated for several months after opening)
White wine	Any good quality Chardonnay
Red wine	Merlot
Port wine	Any variety

Dry Produce to Keep in the Pantry

Onions: Few vegetables are quite as versatile or as essential to the dry produce part of the pantry as onions.

There are two basic types: fresh onions (or sweet onions) and storage onions.

Fresh Onions: These onions come into season in early April and are named after the region in which they are grown. Vidalia come from Georgia, Maui from Hawaii, and 1015 super sweets from Texas. Valued for their sweetness, fresh onions have a high water content and are not hot. Fresh onions have a very short shelf life. Keep them in the refrigerator and use within one week.

Storage Onions: This type of onion is picked at the peak of the summer harvest and dry-cured to help prevent decay. Varieties include yellow, white, Spanish, and red. Shallots are also considered a storage onion. These onions have less water content than the sweet varieties and are quite firm. They have a stronger, more pungent flavor than fresh sweet onions. Red or purple onions, sometimes called Bermuda onions (though not from Bermuda), are among the sweetest and hottest in the category. This onion is an excellent choice for salsa and pico de gallo. Shallots make a good choice when just a small amount of onion is needed. They are great in sauces and salad dressings.

Oils

❋ Nonstick vegetable oil spray. Recommended brand: *Pam*

❋ Extra virgin olive oil for salad dressing and sautéing, stir-frying, and cooking. Olive oil has a strong, somewhat fruity flavor. Buy "extra virgin." Recommended brands: *Da Vinci* and *Colavita*

❋ Canola oil for baking, frying, and sautéing. Canola is mildly flavored and has a high smoke point, which makes it good for sautéing and pan-frying. It can be used as a healthier alternative when vegetable oil is called for in a recipe.

❋ Toasted Asian sesame oil used in Asian cooking. Highly flavored, used in salad dressings and to add a small amount of flavoring to "finish a dish."

❋ Peanut oil for sautéing and frying. Peanut oil has a slightly nutty flavor and a very high heat point, which makes it a good choice for frying.

❋ Other oils as needed. Nut oils such as walnut oil turn rancid quickly. Refrigerate after opening, and taste prior to use. Nut oils are great in salad dressings.

Salts

* Table salt for baking.

* Kosher salt, a coarser grain salt.

* Sea salt for "finishing" the final flavor of a dish.

Sweeteners

* Granulated white sugar, preferably extra-fine

* Light and dark brown, pure cane sugar

* Confectioner's (powdered) sugar

* Maple syrup. Pure grade amber is best. Refrigerate after opening.

* Honey

* Light corn syrup
  Recommended brand: *Karo*

* Molasses

* Sugar substitute
  Recommended brand: *Splenda*

Vinegars

Vinegars vary widely in taste and have a strong flavor impact. Experiment to find those you like.

* Red wine vinegar
  Recommended brands: *Spectrum Naturals Organic* and *Pompeian*

* Sherry vinegar

* Balsamic. Look for an aged, high-quality brand.
  Recommended brand: *Fini,* available at Williams-Sonoma

* Apple cider vinegar
  Recommended brand: *Heinz*

* Distilled white vinegar

Spices and Dried Herbs

* Allspice

* Basil, crumbled

* Bay leaves

* Cayenne pepper

* Celery seed

* Chili powder

* Cinnamon, ground

* Cloves

* Coriander

* Crushed red pepper

- Cumin, ground

- Curry, powdered

- Garlic powder

- Ginger, ground

- Lemon pepper

- Marjoram leaves

- Mustard, dry ground

- Nutmeg, whole. For best flavor, buy nutmeg whole and grate as needed.

- Onion flakes

- Onion powder

- Onion salt

- Oregano leaves

- Paprika

- Parsley

- Peppercorns, whole, black

- Rosemary, crushed

- Sage leaves

- Thyme, crushed

- Tarragon leaves

Herb Blends

- Cajun seasoning

- Greek seasoning
  Recommended brand: *Cavender's*

- Italian seasoning

- *Mrs. Dash*
  (Comes in a variety of blends.)

- *Old Bay* seasoning

- *Lawry's* seasoned salt

Rices

- White

- Brown

- Wild

Storing Smart

When buying dry or canned goods, make sure the dates on the packages or cans haven't expired. Store unopened dry foods in their original packages, and keep opened products in airtight containers.

Food	Storage Time	Special Handling
Baking powder or soda	Check package date	Dry storage.
Bouillon cubes, granules	1 year	Dry storage.
Cake mixes	1 year	Dry storage.
Canned foods, commercial	1 year	Dry storage.
Canola oil	6 months	Keep in a tightly capped bottle, away from heat.
Cereals	Check package date	Keep in airtight container after opening.
Chocolate, baking	1 year	Keep in cool place.
Coconut	6 months	Refrigerate open packages.
Coffee, freshly ground	2 to 3 weeks	Refrigerate or freeze open packages.
Dried pastas	1 year	Keep in airtight container after opening.
Flour, all-purpose	12 months	Cool, dry storage.
Flour, whole wheat	6 months	Refrigerate or freeze during warm weather.
Fruit, dried	6 months	Refrigerate opened packages.
Herbs, dried	9 months	Keep in cool, dark place, and refrigerate red spices.
Honey	1 year	Dry storage.
Jams and jellies	1 year	Refrigerate after opening.

Milk powder, dry, nonfat	6 months	Keep in airtight container after opening.
Molasses	2 years	Dry storage.
Olive oil	4 months	Keep in a tightly capped bottle, away from heat.
Peanut butter	6 months	Refrigerate during warm weather.
Pudding mixes	1 year	Dry storage.
Rice, brown	6 months	Dry storage.
Rice, white	9 months	Keep in an airtight container in a cool place.
Rice, wild	6 months	Dry storage.
Salad dressings, commercial	4 months	Refrigerate open bottles.
Shortening	8 months	Store in a cool place.
Sugar, brown	4 months	Keep in airtight container after opening.
Sugar, granulated	6 months	Keep in an airtight container after opening.
Syrups, corn or maple-flavored	1 year	Refrigerate maple syrup after opening.
Vegetable oil	6 months	Keep in a tightly capped bottle away from heat.
Yeast, active, dry	Check package date	Refrigerate during warm weather.

Timeless Tips

Baking powder is a leavening agent used in baking. Choose an aluminum-free brand, such as *Rumford*. Baking powder has a limited shelf life. An expiration date should be listed on the can. To test if baking powder is good, stir a spoonful into a glass of warm water. Good powder will fizz.

The Refrigerator

A refrigerator is a pantry for cold items, and in the kitchen, the key is organization. Keeping your refrigerator organized helps to keep food fresh and easy to find. Here's how:

Upper Shelf

The upper shelf is a good place for milk and juice cartons (rather than inside the door). To make the most of the space, try to group together items that are similar in height. Store shorter items in the front where you can see them. It helps if you keep like items near one another.

Middle Shelf

The middle shelf is a good place to store cooked foods, casseroles, and leftovers.

Bottom Shelf

The bottom shelf is where you should store packages of meat, chicken, and fish. Put the meat on a rimmed baking sheet to catch any leaks. To prevent eggs from absorbing odors, leave them in their original carton.

Cheese Bin

Many refrigerators come with a special compartment for storing cheese. Besides having temperature control, the drawer prevents odors from spreading to the rest of the refrigerator. If your refrigerator doesn't have a cheese bin, keep wrapped cheeses together in an airtight container.

Door Shelves

Items that aren't likely to spoil (such as jam, mustard, and other condiments) go inside in the door, which is the warmest part of the refrigerator. It's also the easiest spot to reach and is ideal for frequently used items.

Thermometer

To keep your refrigerator at the right temperature (35–39 degrees), place a refrigerator thermometer in the upper front, and adjust the thermostat as needed. Thermometers are inexpensive and are sold at houseware stores and some supermarkets.

Crispers

The cold, dry air of the refrigerator can cause fruits and vegetables to lose moisture quickly. These special bins, sometimes equipped with humidity controls, trap in moisture.

Storing Produce

Never wash vegetables before using as this hastens spoilage. Transfer herbs (these can be washed before storing), salad greens, and other vegetables that need to retain moisture to resealable plastic bags before storing. Most fruits can be kept loose.

Line the Bins

Place several layers of paper towels in the bottom of the crispers to absorb excess moisture and keep the bins clean.

Keeping It Cool

Proper air circulation is necessary to keep foods cool. Don't overload the refrigerator, and don't block the air vents. Also, if you always keep items in the same spot, you won't have to spend time looking for them. Try to avoid leaving the door open for any length of time, as this causes cool air to escape.

Cleaning

Wipe up spills immediately, and make a habit of checking expiration dates and discarding items that are past their prime. To absorb odors, leave an open box of baking soda inside the refrigerator. Every month or so, give the refrigerator a thorough cleaning; work from top to bottom, emptying shelves and bins one at a time and washing them with warm soapy water.

The Freezer

Knowing how to freeze foods will help keep your frozen foods at their optimal quality and taste. No matter how good your aunt's meatloaf might be, it is still going to lose a little flavor when it's stored in the freezer. Improper packaging is the biggest cause of flavor loss, so let's review a few tips before wrapping and freezing.

❈ **Think about it.** Try not to view the freezer as the storage bin between the stove and trash. Freeze only the foods you liked before they were frozen. There are many things you can do to keep soups and casseroles tasting almost as good as they were when they went into the freezer, but no food is going to taste better after it's been frozen and thawed.

❈ **Keep a storage arsenal.** Use containers and wraps designed for the freezer; they are thick enough to keep moisture in and the freezer odors out. Thinner sandwich bags and regular kitchen wrap—even when doubled up—are not durable enough to withstand the big chill. If you are going to freeze anything long-term in glass, make sure the glass is either tempered (the type used for canning jars) or specifically labeled for freezing. Since even freezer-safe glass can crack as food expands, always make sure to leave about 3/4 inch of space between the top of the food and the lid.

❈ **Freeze in small portions.** Whenever possible, pack food in small containers. Large portions in large containers freeze more slowly. The faster the food freezes, the fresher it will taste when it's thawed.

❈ **Slice before you freeze.** Slice bread and halve bagels before freezing one-person servings. Slip bagel halves back-to-back into the freezer bag so that they're less likely to stick together.

- **Squeeze out excess air.** Where there's excess air, there's freezer burn. When you're storing items in a bag such as sliced bread, squeeze out as much air as possible before sealing. When you're storing sauces, soups, or stews in containers, however, leave a bit of space at the top of the container.

- **Stash strategically.** Chill foods first in the refrigerator before you put them in the freezer. Then leave plenty of space around the container in the freezer so the cold air can circulate around it; this will accelerate the freezing. When the item is frozen, go ahead and stack it with everything else.

Freeze Frame

Freezing is an arctic art form. If it is done correctly, you have a good and tasty finished meal. If not, you waste the money spent on the food in the first place. Here are some hints to avoid a tasteless meal.

- **Record before stored.** If the freezer is deep, post a list outside of what's inside. Record the date each item was stored. Use a magnetic pad or an erasable board to record dates and items; or you might use a small spiral pad kept inside a kitchen drawer.

- **Be square.** Use square *Tupperware* whenever possible. Square containers can be stacked and positioned in corners, and they don't take up as much space as round containers.

- **Stack similar foods together.** If you have a side-by-side refrigerator/freezer, designate one shelf for meat, one for baked goods, and one for vegetables.

- **Date your food.** How old is the porridge in storage? Edit the contents of your freezer periodically. Reorganize so the oldest items are always in front so they may be used first.

- **Use shelving.** If you have a freezer on top of your refrigerator, make multi shelves by adding shelf dividers. You can find these dividers at home organization stores.

❀ **Protect meat from freezer burn.** When freezing poultry or meat, first unwrap the item from its original package, and rewrap in freezer paper using freezer tape. Place in a self-sealing freezer bag, such as *Ziploc.* Never freeze meat or poultry in the supermarket packaging. Air leaks in too quickly, ruining the quality of the product.

Freezer Friendly

Your freezer is not just a place to store chili and cookie dough. Think of it as the arctic extension of your pantry—a place to store staples, and even some specialty items—that will make your cooking more efficient and more enjoyable. For optimum results, keep your freezer temperature set to zero degrees.

❀ **Squishable stuff.** Berries, meatballs, hors d'oeuvres, drop cookies, and leftover stuffed pastas (just to name a few) need to be frozen prior to packaging. Spread them out on a baking sheet and freeze until solid, then transfer them to a resealable freezer plastic bag. This method will prevent them from becoming one big, frozen clump.

❀ **Creative cubes.** Use ice cube trays to freeze leftover broth and orange juice. Freeze portions of pesto, tomato paste, and wine (for cooking, not drinking). Once solid, the cubes can be transferred to a resealable freezer bag for safekeeping.

❀ **Casserole capers.** Don't hold the casserole dish hostage in the freezer while you wait to use its contents. Instead, line a casserole dish with foil, assemble the uncooked dish in it, wrap, freeze until solid, and then lift out the foil and the contents. Transfer the block to a freezer bag until you are ready to thaw and cook.

❀ **Edible eggs.** You can freeze eggs as long as they are out of the shell and beaten. Stash yolks and whites separately in resealable plastic bags. If you are freezing only yolks, beat in a pinch of salt or 1/4 teaspoon sugar per egg yolk, to keep them smooth and usable. Choose salt or sugar depending on whether the eggs will be used for a sweet or savory dish. Thaw overnight in the refrigerator. Use 1 tablespoon thawed egg yolk for each fresh egg yolk called for in the recipe.

- **Perfect pancakes.** Let the pancakes or waffles cool, separate with wax paper to prevent sticking, then freeze in resealable plastic freezer bags. To reheat, don't thaw—just pop them in the toaster.

- **Leftover wedding cake.** To preserve frosted cake (a whole cake or a piece), place it in the freezer uncovered until the frosting is firm (about 2 hours, depending on the frosting), then wrap in plastic, then foil. To thaw, unwrap the foil and the plastic, then reshape the foil so it forms a tent over the cake.

- **Nutritious nuts.** Freeze these, as they contain oil that can turn rancid if you keep them in a dry pantry.

- **Cheese choices.** Parmesan, Romano, and aged provolone. Grate them before storing in a resealable freezer bag.

- **Frozen Fruit.** Freeze cubed melon, peaches, mangoes, watermelon, and bananas that are in danger of becoming overripe, and use them to make smoothies or sangria.

What Is Freezer Burn?

Freezer burn occurs when air dries out the surface of foods, toughening the texture and dulling the flavors. The burn is easy to identify. It is frosty and gray. Wrapping foods in airtight, freezer-designed packages can prevent it. Remember, there is nothing unsafe about freezer burn; it reduces the quality of taste, but it will not make anyone sick.

Food	Refrigerator*	Freezer*
Raw meats		
Fresh ground meat	1–2 days	4 months
Chops (lamb)	2–3 days	4 months
Chops (pork)	2–3 days	4 months
Stew meat	1–2 days	4 months
Roasts (beef)	2–3 days	4 months
Roasts (pork, veal)	2–3 days	4 months
Sausage (fresh pork)	1–2 days	2 months
Steaks	3–5 days	6 months
Cooked meats		
Cooked meats, meat dishes	2–3 days	3 months
Processed meats	5 days	1 month
Bacon	1 week	2 months (wrap separately, and pull out what you need)
Ham (fully cooked half)	3–5 days	2 months
Luncheon meats	3–5 days	1 month
Sausage (smoked)	1 week	2 months
Fresh poultry		
Chicken and turkey (whole)	1–2 days	9 months
Chicken pieces	1–2 days	9 months
Duck and goose (whole)	1–2 days	9 months
Turkey pieces	1–2 days	9 months

Cooked poultry

Covered with broth or gravy	1–2 days	6 months
Pieces not in broth gravy	3–4 days	4 months
Cooked casseroles	3–4 days	4 months
Fish	1–2 days	3 months

Eggs

Whites	2–4 days	12 months
Whole eggs (fresh in shell)	3 weeks	Can't freeze
Yolks	2–4 days	12 months

Cheese

Cottage	Refer to use-by date	Can't freeze
Hard cheese	1 month	6 months
Soft cheese	2 weeks	4 months
Ice Cream	Can't refrigerate	2 months
Butter, margarine	1 month	3 months

Dates apply to opened, vacuum-sealed packages. Unopened, vacuum-sealed packages can be stored in refrigerator for 2 weeks or until the use-by or sell-by date expires.

Thawing 101

The flavor and texture of foods you've kept in the freezer can depend on how the foods are defrosted. Slow thawing in the refrigerator is the gentlest and safest method that results in the least change in texture and taste. If you can't wait overnight (or several days for a large piece of meat), there are alternatives.

* **Food safety officer.** Meat, fish, poultry, eggs, and dairy foods should never get warmer than 40 degrees until they are cooked. If you need to thaw them quickly, your best bet is to dunk the bag in cool water. Meat should be completely immersed—you don't want any part exposed to warm air.

* **Marinade magic.** Freeze marinated meats in a resealable bag, and then defrost in the refrigerator overnight. The meat will soak up the marinade as it thaws. This method will also prevent freezer burn on the meat because the liquid "wrap" prevents air from affecting the meat's surface.

* **Mighty microwave.** Use the defrost setting (or 30 percent power) to thaw foods slowly in the microwave. Microwave frozen foods partially covered, and check them every few minutes. Stir whenever possible or turn over and reposition the pieces of meat or fish to ensure even thawing. Remove them from the microwave as soon as they are thawed (they should be flexible and soft but not warm). Always cook thawed foods immediately.

* **Flat freeze.** The greater the surface area, the faster the thaw, so use shallow, flat containers. Freeze broths, sauces, and other liquids flat in freezer bags, and then stand them up sideways for storage. Thaw overnight in the refrigerator.

- **Portion power.** Freeze soups, spaghetti sauce, and lasagna in 1- and 2-portion containers, which thaw more quickly and guarantee you won't thaw more than you need.

- **Refreeze replay**. The flavor may suffer slightly, but you can put defrosted cooked meat, fish, and poultry back into the freezer as long as the meat thawed in the refrigerator and never got warmer than 40 degrees.

Give Me Five

If you keep your cupboard shelves, refrigerator, freezer, vegetable bins, and fruit bowls stocked with the foods on these lists, you will be able to make delicious entrees quickly.

Top Five Pantry Picks:

- Olive oil
- Vinegar (cider, wine, balsamic, rice)
- White and brown rice
- Pasta (several shapes including strand)
- Dried beans

Top Five Can and Jar Goods:

- Canned beans (white, red, black)
- Canned tomatoes (diced and whole plum)
  Recommended brand: *Muir-Glen*
- Canned chicken broth (vegetable and beef)
- Pasta sauce
- Picante sauce

Top Five Baking Items:

* Flour (unbleached, all-purpose)

* Sugar (white, granulated, and light brown)

* Pure vanilla extract

* Semisweet chocolate chips

* Leaveners (baking soda and baking powder)

Top Five Items for the Refrigerator:

* Large eggs

* Milk

* Unsalted butter

* Cheese (soft, such as cream cheese and ricotta; medium, such as cheddar; and hard, such as good-quality Parmesan)

* Cured meat (bacon, prosciutto, ham)

Top Five Items for the Refrigerator Drawers:

* Lettuce (red and green leaf, romaine)

* Bell peppers (green, red)

* Celery

* Carrots

* Fresh herbs (flat leaf parsley, thyme, rosemary)

Top Five Items for the Freezer:

* Frozen vegetables (peas, broccoli, corn, chopped onions)

* Frozen fruit and berries (peaches, raspberries, strawberries, pitted cherries)

* Frozen shrimp (individually quick-frozen—this is very important for optimal taste)

* Frozen chicken parts

* Frozen meatballs

Top Five Items for the Vegetable Basket:

❀ Onions

❀ Garlic

❀ Potatoes (russet and red potatoes) Do not store potatoes in the basket with onions. They shorten each other's shelf life.

❀ Sweet potatoes

❀ Tomatoes

Top Five Items for the Fruit Bowl:

❀ Seasonal fruits (whatever is the best and freshest)

❀ Bananas

❀ Citrus (lemons, limes, and oranges)

❀ Pears

❀ Apples

Top Five Seasonings:

❀ Kosher salt and peppercorns

❀ Dried herbs (bay leaves, marjoram, oregano, thyme, basil)

❀ Dried spices (cumin, cayenne, cinnamon, allspice, cloves)

❀ Chili powder (the best you can find)

❀ Hot pepper sauce

Top Five Asian Ingredients:

❀ Dark toasted sesame oil

❀ Soy sauce (low sodium)

❀ Hoisin sauce

❀ Oyster sauce

❀ Stir-fry sauce

Three Easy Meals
from the Pantry

Skillet Spaghetti

Use this recipe as a good opportunity to experiment with different varieties of pasta sauces.

Serves 4–6

1	28-ounce jar pasta sauce
1 ½	cups water
1	pound Italian-style frozen, fully cooked meatballs
8	ounces thin spaghetti (half of a 16 oz. box), broken in half
1	cup Parmesan cheese, grated

1. In 12-inch skillet, combine spaghetti sauce and water, and stir to combine. Bring to a boil.

2. Add meatballs and broken spaghetti. Stir very well, making sure the spaghetti is under the sauce.

3. Cover, reduce heat, and simmer for 18–20 minutes, stirring every 5 minutes to break up the spaghetti.

4. You may add more water if the mixture appears to be too dry.

5. Cook until spaghetti is *al dente*. Serve with cheese.

Black Bean Soup

Round out this meal by serving corn or flour tortillas. For dessert add fresh orange slices drizzled with honey and topped with a dash of cinnamon.

Serves 4

1	tablespoon canola oil
1	cup of chopped fresh or frozen onion
2	cloves garlic, minced
2	15-ounce cans of black beans, rinsed and drained
1	14 ½-ounce can of diced tomatoes, undrained
1	14-ounce can of chicken broth
1/2	cup picante sauce
1/4	cup water
1	teaspoon of ground cumin
2	tablespoons of lime juice
	fresh cilantro (garnish)
	sour cream (garnish)

1. In a large saucepan, heat oil over medium heat. Add onion and garlic, and sauté 5 minutes, or until tender.

2. Stir in beans and next five ingredients. Bring to a boil; reduce heat and simmer uncovered for 15 minutes.

3. Remove from heat, and stir in lime juice.

4. Ladle soup into bowls, and garnish with cilantro and sour cream, if desired.

Cook's notes:

Substitute 1/2 teaspoon of garlic powder for fresh garlic, if desired.

For additional flavor, substitute one 14 ½-ounce can of diced fire-roasted or Mexican tomatoes for the regular can of diced tomatoes called for in the recipe.

Red Beans and Rice

This is a great meal to pull together when you are snuggled up at home and don't feel like venturing out.

Serves 4

1	tablespoon canola oil
1	onion, chopped
1	small green bell pepper, seeded and chopped
2	cloves garlic, minced
1	8-ounce can tomato sauce
1/2	teaspoon dried oregano leaves
1/2	teaspoon dried thyme leaves
1/8	teaspoon cayenne pepper
1	teaspoon of Cajun seasoning
1	7-ounce package red beans and rice mix

1. In a heavy skillet over medium heat, sauté onion, bell pepper, and garlic in olive oil until tender.

2. Add all remaining ingredients except red beans and rice mix, and simmer over low heat for 10 minutes to blend flavors.

3. Prepare red beans and rice mix as directed on package, and combine with tomato and onion mixture.

4. Simmer for 3–5 minutes longer to blend flavors.

Cook's note:

For a heartier version, sauté some smoked sausage along with the onion mixture.

Stew-pendous Souper Supper

Menu

New Year's Day Soup

Bottle o' Beer Stew

Apple, Cheese, and Nut Salad

Garden Vegetable Marinade

Confetti Corn Bread

Butterscotch Brownies

Too many brews spoil the cook.

—Anonymous

A brand new year is similar to an artist's blank canvas—a beautiful picture is just waiting to happen! What picture will you paint? What traditions will you start? A new year is full of potential, and it awaits our personal touches. Sharing the first day of the year with friends and family is a spectacular start to a new beginning. Happy New Year!

Wine Time

For a boisterous gathering celebrating the New Year, matching a hearty menu of bold flavors would include serving the same amber beer, such as Bass Ale, used in the Bottle o' Beer Stew, and an uncomplicated, sturdy red wine such as a French Cotes du Rhone (Guigal), Spanish Rioja (Marqués de Riscal), or California Petite Sirah (Jewel). Offer a white wine with body enough for this substantial menu, such as an Australian Chardonnay (Rosemount Roxburgh) or Chilean Sauvignon Blanc (Casa Lapostolle from the family who produces Grand Marnier). And don't overlook a sparkling wine (Mumm or Domaine Chandon) for toasting the New Year, if that fits in with your plans for an open house!

New Year's Day Soup

Hearty soups and stews are a perfect main course for the "first supper" of the New Year. As they simmer on the stove, the aroma leads your guests to the table.

In the South, tradition says that eating black-eyed peas on the first day of the year brings good luck and prosperity, so get a heaping helping.

Serves 8

1	tablespoon canola oil
1/2	medium onion, chopped
2	cloves garlic, minced
1	cup ham, cooked and diced
1/2	green bell pepper, seeded and chopped
1	carrot, peeled and sliced
6	cups water
1	10-ounce can mild **Rotel** tomatoes
1	14 ½-ounce can chicken broth
1/2	pound dried black-eyed peas, sorted and rinsed
1/2	teaspoon freshly ground pepper
1	teaspoon salt

1. In a large 6- or 8-quart stockpot, heat oil over medium heat. Add onions, bell pepper, garlic, and ham. Sauté until vegetables are soft and ham is slightly brown.

2. Add remaining ingredients.

3. Cook until the peas are tender, about 1 ½ hours.

Cook's note:

If you need a small amount of ham, buy an already-cooked ham steak and dice it up. Packaged ham steaks are found in the supermarket near the lunch meats.

How to Chop, Dice, and Mince Onion

1. Cut off the stem, then cut the onion in half through the root.

2. Peel off the skin.

3. Place one of the halves, flat-side down, on the cutting board.

4. Make parallel lengthwise cuts. DON'T cut through the root end.

5. Cut horizontal slices from top to bottom.

6. Make pieces as thick or thin as desired: thick cuts equal chopped; medium cuts equal diced; thin cuts equal minced.

7. Cut off the root.

Reduce or Prevent Tears When Chopping

Sulfuric compounds in onion cells are released into the air when an onion is chopped. This irritates the eyes and causes them to release tears. The way to avoid this problem is by doing BOTH of the following: 1) freeze the onion for 20 minutes before you chop it (a cold onion won't release sulfuric compounds as readily as a warm one), and 2) always leave the root end of the onion intact while you chop (the sulfuric compounds are concentrated there).

Making the Cut

Chop, dice, and mince. What these techniques are and how they differ can be confusing. Here's a quick guide to help you.

* For chopped food, think of gambling dice, roughly 1/2 x 1/2 inch; a large cut would be 3/4 x 3/4 inch. It's a good cut to use when making dishes that cook awhile, such as stews, soups, and stocks.

* When dicing, keep a pencil eraser in mind, 1/4–3/8 x 1/4–3/8 inch. If something is to be sautéed for short periods of time or eaten raw, as in salsa, then use a small dice.

* Mincing is just cutting food into tiny bits. When you mince garlic or shallots, the small pieces spread throughout a dish, permeating it with flavor. To mince, first roughly chop or dice the food, then rock your knife back and forth over it until the bits are very small.

Bottle o' Beer Stew

A savory stew is a complete meal. Warming from the inside out, this healthy and delicious stew adds another dimension to complete the party.

Serves 6–8

1/2	cup all-purpose flour
1/2	teaspoon salt
1/2	teaspoon freshly ground pepper
2	pounds beef stew meat, cut into 1 ½-inch cubes
2	tablespoons canola oil
1	large onion, chopped
2	cloves garlic, minced
1	12-ounce bottle of amber beer
1	14-ounce can low-sodium beef broth
1	28-ounce can diced tomatoes (*Muir Glen* fire-roasted style)
2	medium carrots, cut into 1/2-inch pieces
4	medium red potatoes, not peeled, cut into 3/4-inch slices
1	cup frozen peas

1. Place the flour, salt, and pepper in a large, resealable plastic bag. Close and shake to combine. Add half the stew meat; close and shake to coat the meat with the flour mixture.

2. In a 5-quart Dutch oven, heat oil over medium-high heat. Remove the meat from the plastic bag, shaking off excess flour. Add the meat chunks to the hot oil, and brown on all sides. Remove meat from the oil, and set aside.

3. Repeat the process, coating the remaining half of the meat and browning it, adding a little more oil to the pot if needed. Remove the meat from the pot, add onion and garlic, and sauté 2 minutes, stirring to prevent burning.

4. Add the browned meat back into the pot, along with the beer, broth, and tomatoes, stirring to combine. Cover the pot with a heavy lid, bring to a boil, turn down the heat to low, and simmer for 1 hour.

5. Remove the cover, stir in the carrots and potatoes, and continue simmering over low heat, uncovered, for another hour or until the meat is very tender and the stew is dark in color. Stir in peas, simmer 10 minutes, and add salt and pepper to taste. Serve.

Garlic Time

1. Peel the garlic by placing it on the cutting board, whacking it with the side of the your chef's knife, and then slipping off the skin.

2. Holding the chef's knife in one hand, steady the garlic clove on the cutting board with the other, leaning the knuckles of your index and middle fingers against the blade. Keep your fingertips folded inward to prevent cutting yourself.

3. Using mostly the tip of your knife, work your chef's knife up and down, slowly moving your knuckles toward the other end of the garlic as you chop. This method takes practice!

4. Do not over-brown garlic when sautéing in a skillet. It will taste bitter, and you will have to throw it out and start over.

Confetti Corn Bread

Corn bread is a must have with soups and stews. Its coarse texture and tasty flavor make this the perfect accompaniment to your meal.

Ease in preparation is often just the ticket to keep your meal-prep time to a minimum. This quick recipe adds delicious mix-ins to spice up the mix. Refer to November for the scratch recipe.

Serves 4–6

1   8 ½-ounce box corn bread mix
      (*Jiffy* corn muffin mix)

1   large egg

1/3   cup milk

1/3   cup sharp cheddar cheese, grated

1/4   cup corn (canned or frozen)

1. Preheat oven to 400 degrees.

2. In a small bowl, blend corn bread mix, egg, and 1/3 cup milk. Stir to combine.

3. Sprinkle grated cheese and corn over the batter, and stir to combine. Batter will be slightly lumpy.

4. Pour batter into a greased, square, 8x8 *Pyrex* pan, or into an 8-inch, cast-iron skillet. If using the skillet, put in 1 tablespoon butter, and preheat until the butter is melted and sizzles slightly. This will produce a crisp, golden crust.

5. Bake 20–25 minutes. Cool slightly, then slice and serve with butter.

Apple, Cheese, and Nut Salad

Apples have a healthful magic packed in a crunchy bite. Mix up a power potion by adding cheese, nuts, and freshly squeezed juice. This salad is a light accompaniment to soups and stews.

Serves 4–6

3	large red apples, unpeeled and chopped
2	tablespoons fresh-squeezed orange juice
1	cup seedless green grapes, halved
1/2	cup celery, chopped
1/2	cup walnuts, chopped
1/2	cup mild cheddar cheese, cubed
1/4	cup sunflower seeds
1/2	teaspoon freshly grated orange peel
1/3	cup good-quality mayonnaise (not salad dressing)

1. In a medium bowl, place chopped apples and sprinkle them with orange juice.

2. Add grapes, celery, walnuts, sunflower seeds, cheese, orange zest, and mayonnaise to chopped apples. Mix until well combined.

3. Serve in a purple cabbage leaf.

Garden Vegetable Marinade

Crunchy vegetables and soft, juicy tomatoes marinated in a herb-filled sauce add taste, style, and freshness to your New Year's Day menu.

Serves 4–6

2	cups each broccoli and cauliflower florets
1	cup cherry tomatoes, cut in half
1	medium carrot, cut into 1/8-inch slices

Marinade:

1/3	cup cider vinegar
1/4	cup extra virgin olive oil
1	clove garlic, minced
1	teaspoon dried thyme
1	tablespoon fresh dill or 1 teaspoon dried dill weed
1/2	teaspoon salt
1/4	teaspoon pepper

1. In a medium bowl, combine vegetables.

2. In a small bowl, combine all marinade ingredients. Whisk to blend.

3. Pour marinade over vegetables, and gently toss to coat.

4. Cover and refrigerate 1–2 hours, stirring occasionally.

Salad Bar Star

If you need small amounts of a vegetable—such as broccoli florets or cherry tomatoes—for a recipe, use your supermarket's salad bar.

Butterscotch Brownies

This recipe is a real winner! I brought home the State Fair of Texas blue-ribbon prize for the brownie bake-off after entering this dessert several years ago. Simple yet succulent, it's just right for mixing in your favorite morsels, nuts, or candies.

Yield: about 1 ½ dozen

1	cup unsalted butter, softened to room temperature
2	teaspoons vanilla extract
2	tablespoons molasses
2 ½	cups packed light brown sugar
4	large eggs
2	cups all-purpose flour
1 ½	cup pecans, chopped

1. Preheat oven to 350 degrees.

2. In a large bowl, beat the butter, vanilla extract, and molasses until well combined.

3. Add sugar and beat well.

4. Add eggs one at a time, beating after each addition. Beat until mixture is smooth and light in color.

5. Stir in flour and nuts.

6. Place in a 13x9x2-inch greased baking pan. Bake for 30–35 minutes, or until a toothpick inserted in the middle comes out almost clean.

Cook's note:

Mix in 1 cup butterscotch morsels or 1 cup toffee bits. You can also use walnuts or macadamia nuts in place of the pecans.

Easy Lining

To easily lift brownies from the pan, line pan with foil. Turn pan upside down and mold foil over bottom, leaving 3 inches extending over the short sides. Place pre-formed foil into pan, and crunch down extended sides to form handles. Use handles to lift brownies from pan after baking. This technique will ensure even, pretty cuts.

Parties with Panache

※ BYOB (Bring Your Own Bowl) New Year's Day party. What fun it is to see different bowls with their interesting colors, shapes, and textures. They will add such interest to your service area and will be quite a conversation starter.

※ Purchase a variety of beer, remove from the cartons, place the bottles or cans in a large washtub, and ice them down. If you do not have a washtub, place the ice in a clean sink or cooler; even your washing machine will work in a pinch. To drain, program your washer for the final spin cycle.

※ Beer comes in fun and interesting cartons that can make a festive decoration. Fold the beer cartons to flatten. Tape cartons together end to end. Use it as a table runner on your buffet or dinner table.

※ Assorted colorful blankets make great tablecloths.

※ Candles, candles, candles—set the mood. Make sure the scent is light so as not to overpower your foods.

※ Place a few of your side dishes in clean, galvanized buckets to create a rustic, yet relaxed feel.

An Evening of Elegance

Menu

Beef Filets with Cherry Sauce

Fresh Herbed Red Potatoes

Winter Salad with
Herbed Red Wine Vinaigrette

Garlic Popovers

Cappuccino Trifles for Two

Sweetheart Truffles

Bread and wine and thou; it is all here.

—Barry Benepe, Director, Greenmarkets

Romance is love's finest hour. Creating a comfortable and relaxing candlelight dinner for two is a perfect way to celebrate Valentine's Day. Approach your evening by addressing all the senses, and make a delicious dining experience extra special.

Sight. Look at your surroundings. Try moving your breakfast table into the den in front of the fireplace. Cover the table with your favorite tablecloth, or purchase a couple of yards of red velvet from your fabric shop and transform it into a table covering. Use your sparkling new china and stemware. Sprinkle white and pink rose petals all around the table. Add a pair of crystal candlesticks to the top of your table. This will add an elegant touch with just the right amount of light.

Sound. Select your favorite CDs for background music.

Touch. Use soft napkins and comfortable chairs.

Taste. The menu was created with variety in mind. Combining several courses with fresh herbs, fruits, chocolate, and coffee, one cannot go wrong.

Smell. Orange rind, cinnamon sticks, and cloves stirred into a prepared apple cider and simmered gently on top of the stove create a quick, no-need-for-measurement aroma that will fill your home.

Comfort. You know what is comfortable for you both. Keep comfort and your senses in mind as you celebrate your love.

Wine Time

An intimate dinner for two calls for pulling out all the stops! Precede your meal with a split (a half bottle) of sparkling wine, such as Mionetto Prosecco. Look for a Blanc de Noir from California or France (Schramsberg). Consider a bold red for the main course, such as a Pinot Noir from Oregon (King Estate or Duck Pond) or a Cabernet Sauvignon from California (Kenwood Jack London). If you're going to linger over dessert, look for a chilled split of dessert wine—a late-harvest German Beerenauslese (from Riesling grapes) or a late-harvest California Muscat (Bonny Doon). For this special menu, you might want to consult with a trusted and dependable wine merchant.

Beef Filets with Cherry Sauce

These tender filets slice like warm butter. Topped with sweet and savory cherries, the subtle but distinctive flavors will enhance your romantic evening.

Serves 2

2	4-ounce beef tenderloin steaks
1/2	cup port wine
1/2	cup halved, frozen, dark, pitted cherries, unsweetened, thawed
1 ½	teaspoons stone-ground mustard
1	teaspoon Worcestershire sauce
3/4	teaspoon cornstarch

Variations:

Cranberry juice can be used instead of the port. Another meat option: 1 pork tenderloin, 3/4 pound. Cut tenderloin into 1 ¼-inch thick pieces. Sprinkle with salt and pepper. Cook pork in small amount of oil, over medium-high heat, for 3–4 minutes on each side, remove from skillet, then add the meat back to the sauce, as instructed in step 6.

1. Season beef with salt and freshly ground pepper.

2. Lightly coat a nonstick skillet with cooking spray.

3. Brown steaks over medium-high heat. Remove from skillet.

4. In a small bowl, stir together port, stone-ground mustard, Worcestershire sauce, and cornstarch.

5. Place the port mixture in the skillet, and stir 1–2 minutes, or until thickened. Add cherries, and bring mixture to a simmer.

6. Add the steaks, and cook 4–5 minutes or until meat reaches desired doneness.

Fresh Herbed Red Potatoes

Potatoes and fresh creamy butter—a match made in heaven! This duo makes a fabulous debut when tossed with fresh herbs. Select your favorite herb combination to create your own special tastes.

Serves 2–3

1	pound small red potatoes
1/2	tablespoon butter
1	green onion, sliced
1	clove garlic, minced
1/2	tablespoon parsley leaves, minced
1	teaspoon fresh chives, snipped
1/4	teaspoon salt
1/8	teaspoon freshly ground pepper

1. Wash potatoes in cool water.
2. With a vegetable peeler, peel a ring around the centers of the potatoes.
3. In a small sauce pan, cover potatoes with water; simmer for about 20 minutes.
4. Drain and transfer the potatoes to a bowl.
5. In a small skillet over medium-low heat, melt butter.
6. Add green onions, garlic, parsley, chives, salt, and pepper.
7. Cook until the garlic is fragrant.
8. Gently stir the mixture into the potatoes.

Tater Talk

What Are New Potatoes?

Any variety of potato that is harvested early is considered a new potato. Since they are picked before their sugars have converted to starch, new potatoes are waxy and high in moisture. They also have thin skins, making them great for cooking and eating unpeeled.

Buying and Storing

New potatoes should be firm, smooth, and free of cracks or soft brown spots. Choose potatoes of similar size so they cook evenly. Potatoes should not be refrigerated. Keep them in a cool, dark place, and use them within several weeks of buying.

Cooking

The waxy flesh helps new potatoes hold their shape when cooked (they should be tender when pierced with a knife), making them ideal for soups and potato salads. If potatoes are to be cooked in their skins, rinse under cool water, scrub with a vegetable brush, and cut away any greenish parts.

European Winter Salad with Red Wine Vinaigrette

Kick up the flavor of a midwinter salad by topping it with candied walnuts and feta cheese.

Serves 2–3

1/2	head red leaf or Bibb lettuce
1	cup mixed European field greens
1	small red plum, sliced
2	green onions, chopped
1/4	cup candied walnuts
1/4	cup crumbled feta cheese

Vinaigrette

3	tablespoons red wine vinegar
1/2	teaspoon dried marjoram
1/2	teaspoon sugar
1/4	teaspoon salt
1/4	teaspoon freshly ground pepper
1/4	cup extra virgin olive oil

1. In a medium bowl, toss together all salad ingredients.

2. In a small bowl, mix red wine vinegar, marjoram, sugar, salt, and pepper.

3. Slowly whisk in the olive oil.

4. Let the mixture sit at room temperature for 30 minutes so the flavors can blend.

5. Toss vinaigrette with salad greens, and top with crumbled feta and walnuts.

Garlic Popovers

Light, airy, and unique, these popovers will look gorgeous on your plate. They are fun to eat and a snap to prepare.

Yield: 4

1/2	cup milk
1	large egg
1/2	cup all-purpose flour
1/4	teaspoon salt
1/4	teaspoon garlic powder or Italian herb blend

1. Preheat oven to 425 degrees

2. In a small bowl, combine the milk and egg.

3. Add flour, salt, and garlic powder (or Italian herb blend) to milk and egg mixture. Using a handheld electric mixer, beat until smooth.

4. Pour 1/3 cup of the batter into four well-greased (6-ounce) custard cups.

5. Place cups on a baking sheet. Bake for 15 minutes, then turn the oven down to 350 degrees. (Don't open the oven door.) Continue to bake for 15–20 minutes, or until the popovers are a deep, golden brown.

Sweetheart Truffles

Easy, yet impressive, these make-ahead truffles will disappear quickly. Rich chocolate—rolled in nuts for a crunch—will add just the right look and taste to your fancy feast.

Yield: 1 dozen

1/4	cup heavy whipping cream
1 ½	teaspoons butter
1/4	teaspoon vanilla extract
2	1.55-ounce milk chocolate candy bars
2	1-ounce squares semisweet chocolate, chopped
1/3	cup almonds or pecans, finely chopped

Cook's notes:

To make mint truffles, add 1/4 teaspoon of peppermint extract instead of vanilla, and roll balls in crushed peppermints.

Topping ideas: cocoa powder, crushed toffee chips, flaked coconut.

*For testing purposes in this recipe, **Ghirardelli** semisweet chocolate and **Hershey's** milk chocolate candy bars were used.*

1. In a small saucepan over low heat, warm cream and butter until small bubbles form on top and the butter is melted.

2. Remove from heat, and add vanilla, candy bars, and semisweet chocolate.

3. Stir until smooth.

4. Quickly transfer the mixture to a small stainless steel or glass bowl.

5. Press plastic wrap onto the surface of the chocolate mixture. This seals out the air and keeps a rubbery film from forming.

6. Refrigerate for 2 hours, or until easy to handle.

7. Scoop out a heaping teaspoon of chocolate mixture and using the palm of your hand, roll mixture into a ball. Roll the balls in nuts. Refrigerate for 2 hours or until firm. Store truffles in the refrigerator.

Chocolate Storage

Keep These Tips in Mind When Storing Chocolate

* Chocolate chips, baking chocolate, and candy coating stay fresh for at least a year if kept in a cool, dry place (60–70 degrees).

* Since chocolate absorbs odors readily, it should be wrapped and stored separately from strongly flavored foods.

* The gray film that sometimes appears on chocolate is called bloom. It occurs when chocolate undergoes varying temperatures, which causes the cocoa butter to rise to the surface and create the film. Bloom has no affect on the taste or quality of the chocolate.

Perfect Whipped Cream

Whipped Cream. All it takes is a bowl and a whisk (or electric mixer) and a few minutes of your time. A sweet, fluffy dollop of whipped cream on a piece of pie, spooned onto shortcakes or layered in parfaits, is the perfect topper.

Here's How:

1. Chill bowl, whisk, or electric mixer attachments until well chilled. Don't skip this step; it's very important to have utensils and cream very cold for producing stiff peaks. In a deep mixing bowl, beat 1 cup heavy cream until soft peaks form.

2. Sprinkle 1–2 tablespoons granulated sugar over cream. Beat until stiff peaks form. Do not overbeat, or you will have butter instead of whipped cream. Makes about 2 cups.

Cook's note:

If you prefer, you can replace the granulated sugar with an equal amount of confectioner's sugar. To prevent any lumps from forming, use a fine-mesh sieve to sift the sugar over the cream.

Cappuccino Trifles for Two

Decadent! This dessert is a refreshing, sweet end to a meaningful celebration. Trifles for two are a great exchange for a delicious accompaniment to the traditional after-dinner coffee.

Serves 2

1	3-ounce package cream cheese, softened to room temperature
2	teaspoons sugar
4	teaspoons crème caramel coffee drink mix, or any other flavored, sweetened, instant coffee or cappuccino powder mix
1	tablespoon milk
1	cup whipping cream, whipped
1	tablespoon sugar
1/4	cup caramel syrup
2	slices pound cake, cut into cubes

1. In a small bowl using a handheld electric mixer, beat cream cheese, coffee powder, sugar, and milk until smooth.

2. In a separate mixing bowl, beat whipping cream with 1 tablespoon sugar until soft peaks form. Gently fold into the cream cheese mixture.

3. Divide the pound cake cubes between two parfait glasses.

4. Drizzle with caramel syrup or any coffee liqueur.

5. Top with cream cheese mixture and chocolate chips.

6. To the top of each parfait glass, add a dollop of whipped cream.

Parties with Panache

❀ Red and white netting atop your dining table turns an ordinary meal into a festive occasion. This is an inexpensive way to add pizzazz.

❀ Fill different-sized clear glass bowls with pink and red M&Ms—a clever and delicious way to add color and holiday fun around your home.

❀ Fill a glass cylinder with conversation hearts. Festive and tasty!

❀ Purchase some colorful heart-shaped boxes at a discount store. Stack them in threes around your home.

❀ Wrap a little gift in foil. Place your gift in the center of two pieces of foil. Fold the foil up and around your gift. Twist the top to resemble a large chocolate kiss. A simple white piece of paper, cut into a thin rectangle and stuck into the slit in the top of the package, works as your card.

Spring Salad Supper

Menu

Steak Caesar Salad for Two

Raspberry Salad
with Grilled Chicken

Monterey Chicken Salad

Splendid Sauces for
Ice Cream and Cakes

Cauliflower is nothing but cabbage with a college education.

—Mark Twain

Let's hear it for the best-kept secret in supermarket produce—packaged lettuces in numerous varieties. Rinse your mix with cool water to keep the leaves cool and crisp. Add fruity, savory, or traditional dressings to your bowl, top with tasty steak or chicken, and you have created a marvelous meal.

Wine Time

Rich with assertive flavors, the steak Caesar salad calls for a California Zinfandel (Renwood), Italian Chianti (Antinori Classico), or another Sangiovese (Valley of the Moon). The fruity background of raspberry salad with grilled chicken pairs with a New Zealand Sauvignon Blanc (Villa Maria) or a rosé from California (Preston). With its bold southwestern flavors and ingredients, Monterey chicken salad pairs nicely with Italian Chianti or another Sangiovese (see suggestions above), a Spanish Rioja (Marqués de Riscal), or a German Riesling (Christoffel Urziger Wurzgarten).

Steak Caesar Salad for Two

Steak salad is a winner, especially when served as a hearty main dish. Toss the steak salad with a tasty, fresh Caesar dressing, and dinner has become a fabulous treat.

Serves 2

1	tablespoon lemon pepper seasoning
2	boneless sirloin strip steaks (3/4-inch thick), trimmed
5	cups romaine lettuce
1/4	cup croutons (see recipe on page 101)
1/4	cup Caesar salad dressing (see recipe on page 96)
6	cherry tomatoes, halved

1. Preheat broiler—low setting. (For easy cleanup, line broiler pan with foil or buy disposable foil broiler pans.)

2. Rub lemon pepper seasoning on both sides of the steak. Place steak on broiler pan that has been coated with cooking spray.

3. Broil 2–3 minutes on each side, or until meat reaches desired doneness.

4. Combine lettuce, cherry tomatoes, and Caesar dressing in a large bowl. Toss gently. Arrange on two dinner plates.

5. Slice steak into thin strips, and arrange evenly over the lettuce. Add selected crouton garnish evenly over the top of the salad.

Variation:

Steak can be grilled

Caesar Dressing

Fresh is best, and this easy-to-prepare dressing adds a flavor pop to your greens.

Yield: 1/2 cup

1	clove garlic, chopped
1/8	teaspoon salt
1/4	cup Parmesan cheese, finely grated
1	tablespoon fresh lemon juice
1	tablespoon mayonnaise
1	teaspoon anchovy paste
1	teaspoon Dijon mustard
1	teaspoon Worcestershire sauce
1/4	cup extra virgin olive oil
	salt and freshly cracked pepper to taste

1. Sprinkle salt over chopped garlic and mince, forming a paste. Place in a small bowl.

2. Add Parmesan cheese, lemon juice, mayonnaise, anchovy paste, Dijon mustard, and Worcestershire sauce. Stir until blended.

3. Whisk in oil in a slow, steady stream.

4. Season with salt and freshly cracked pepper. Chill.

Nice Slice

With a simple flourish, sliced tomatoes become an attractive salad or appetizer. Try topping the slices with:

❋ Bottled corn relish.

❋ A slice of mozzarella, chopped fresh basil, and a drizzle of extra virgin olive oil.

❋ Chopped fresh cucumber blended with fresh dill and vinaigrette.

❋ Crumbled blue cheese and toasted pine nuts.

Raspberry Salad with Grilled Chicken

Sweet raspberries add a flavorful dimension to a grilled chicken salad. Marinating the chicken in a unique, fruity, sweet-and-sour vinaigrette gives the dish a delicious twist.

Serves 4

4	boneless and skinless chicken breasts
4	cups baby spinach
4	cups leaf lettuce
1	cup raspberries or strawberries, halved
4	tablespoons feta cheese
3	tablespoons toasted almonds, sliced
1/4	cup purple onion, thinly sliced

Raspberry Vinaigrette

1/3	cup raspberry jam (*Simply Fruit*)
1/3	cup balsamic vinegar
1/3	cup raspberry wine vinegar
1	teaspoon red wine vinegar
1/4	cup extra virgin olive oil
1/2	package dry Italian salad dressing mix (*Good Seasons*)

1. In a small bowl, combine all of the vinaigrette ingredients. Stir thoroughly to combine.

2. Place chicken breasts in a glass casserole dish, and spoon the vinaigrette over each piece, reserving some for the salad. Marinate for 30 minutes to 1 hour.

3. Grill or bake the chicken. Cool slightly and slice on the diagonal.

4. In a medium bowl, combine salad greens, raspberries or strawberries, and purple onion. Add remaining dressing. Gently toss.

5. Divide the greens mixture among four plates. Place sliced chicken on top of the greens. Sprinkle with feta cheese and sliced almonds.

Cook's notes:

If the baking method is used, bake in a 375 degree oven for about 25 minutes.

Monterey Chicken Salad

Colorful and spicy, the perfect combo of vegetables will make this salad a regular on your menu. Toss with a salsa-and-ranch dressing, and dinner is ready on the double!

Serves 4

2	tablespoons canola oil
1	pound packaged chicken breast tenders, diced
1/2	package taco seasoning
1	prepared bag iceberg lettuce, such as **(Fresh Express Iceberg Garden)**
1	cup corn, canned or frozen (defrosted if frozen)
1	cup black beans, rinsed and drained
1	avocado, peeled and diced
1	cup Monterey Jack cheese, grated
1	small tomato, diced
	crushed tortilla chips for garnish

Dressing

1/2	cup ranch dressing
1/4	cup salsa

1. In a large skillet, heat oil over medium-high heat. Add the diced chicken tenders, and sprinkle them with taco seasoning.

2. Sauté until cooked through and brown.

3. In a large bowl, place the salad greens, corn, and black beans. Toss to combine.

4. Add the seasoned, cooked chicken to the top of the salad mixture.

5. Top with diced avocado and Monterey Jack cheese.

6. In a small bowl, combine ranch dressing and salsa.

7. Toss salad with the dressing.

8. Garnish with crushed tortilla chips.

Honey Lemon Dressing

Yield: 1/4 cup

1/4	cup fresh lemon juice
2	tablespoons honey
1	tablespoon extra virgin olive oil
1/8	teaspoon of salt
1/8	teaspoon freshly ground black pepper

1. In a small bowl, place all ingredients.
2. Whisk to combine.

Fruit and Cheese

Fruit and cheese combinations are a match made in heaven.

Classic fruit and cheese combinations:

1. Apples with blue cheese.
2. Strawberry halves and orange sections with feta cheese.
3. Sliced pear with Brie or goat cheese.

Salad Garnishes

Fresh Herbs

Toss your favorite fresh herbs with your salad greens. Many herbs have strong flavors. Use them sparingly so that the delicate flavors of the greens are not overpowered. Use edible flowers to add color, flavor, and aroma.

Terrific Toppers

These different toppers will add flavor, crunch, and eye appeal to your salad creations.

Parmesan Cheese Toast

Yield: *varies with baguette size*

       French bread baguette

1/4 –1/2   cup Parmesan cheese

       olive oil

1. Preheat oven to its lowest broiler setting.

2. Cut the baguette into 1/2-inch thick slices.

3. Brush bread slices with olive oil, then sprinkle with Parmesan cheese.

4. Arrange bread slices on a baking sheet, and broil 1 minute, or until the cheese begins to melt. Watch closely because these can burn quickly.

Puff Pastry Croutons

Yield: *varies*

1   3x3x¼–inch piece of puff pastry

1. Using a mini cookie cutter of your choice, cut the puff pastry into small shapes.

2. Preheat oven to 425 degrees. Bake on a cookie sheet until golden and crisp.

Homemade Croutons

Yield: 3 ½ cups

3	cups 1/2-inch cubes French bread
2	tablespoons canola oil
1	clove garlic, minced
1/4	cup Parmesan cheese, finely grated
1/2	teaspoon dried basil
1/4	teaspoon dried thyme
1/4	teaspoon onion powder

1. Preheat oven to 350 degrees.

2. In a small bowl, combine oil and minced garlic.

3. In a small bowl, place the cubed French bread. Mix in the Parmesan and herbs.

4. Pour the oil and garlic mixture over the bread cubes; toss to combine.

5. Spread the bread cubes in a single layer on a pan with a rim (15x10x1-inch baking pan). Line the pan with foil or parchment paper for easy cleanup.

6. Bake until dry and lightly browned, about 15–20 minutes.

Cook's notes:

Parchment paper is a professional cook's secret for easy cleanup! The paper is grease-proof and silicone-coated, so it won't stick or burn. Use for lining cookie sheets or placing over foods in the microwave—the paper will save you time and effort.

Get creative with your bread choice. Try Artesian bread with nuts for a heartier crouton, or sourdough for a little bit of a zing. Pair with hearty greens like romaine. Store in a paper lunch bag on the countertop, not in the refrigerator.

Green Scene

Boston and Bibb are two of the most popular butterhead lettuces. They are soft and pliable and have a buttery texture and flavor. Their leaves form cups when separated from the heads. These lettuces work wonderfully for wraps or for holding any type of fruit or combined salads.

Leaf lettuce has both red and green leaves with bright colors, mild flavors, and tender textures. Good quality leaf lettuce should have nicely shaped leaves free of bruises, breaks, or brown spots.

Romaine is hearty and crisp, not bitter. Romaine has enough structure to stand up to strongly flavored dressings (like Caesar). A good head of romaine has dark green outer leaves, and no yellowing or bruises.

Mesclun contains a mixture of several kinds of baby lettuces.

Arugula has a strong, spicy, peppery flavor. This variety is not good alone, but it adds a zip when tossed with other greens.

Radicchio has a bitter flavor and a pretty purple color. This variety should be used sparingly, mixed with other greens.

Iceberg is the most common of all lettuce varieties, and is mildly flavored. Iceberg stays crisp for a long time. Select heads that are firm but not hard.

Fresh Herbs and Greens

Serves 4

3	cups mesclun (baby salad greens)
3	cups romaine lettuce, torn
1/4	cup thinly sliced red onion
3	tablespoons fresh Italian parsley, chopped
2	tablespoons fresh basil, chopped
1	cup cherry or teardrop tomatoes (if using cherry tomatoes, cut them in half)

Vinaigrette

1	tablespoon minced shallots
2	tablespoons sherry vinegar
3	tablespoons extra virgin olive oil
1/8	teaspoon salt
1/4	teaspoon Dijon mustard
1/8	teaspoon fresh ground black pepper

1. In a small bowl, combine shallots and vinegar. Let stand for 5 minutes. Slowly whisk in oil.

2. Add mustard, salt, and pepper. Whisk to combine.

3. In a large bowl, place salad greens, onion, fresh herbs, and tomatoes. Toss gently to combine. Drizzle the vinaigrette over the salad. Toss lightly to coat.

Cook's notes:

Let your imagination be your guide for add-ins such as nuts, dried cranberries, and pumpkin seeds.

Be generous with your measurement of salad greens.

Preparing and Storing Salad Greens

Preparing

All lettuces and other salad greens should be washed first. Wash again in a bowl of clean water after they have been torn or cut. Dry with a salad spinner, or blot with a paper towel. Dry thoroughly because wet salad greens repel oil-based dressings and dilute their flavors.

Storing

For quick salads, keep greens washed, dried, and wrapped in a paper towel. Store in a plastic resealable bag in the refrigerator. Do not store greens with tomatoes or apples because the ethylene gas that they produce will cause the greens to wilt and accelerate spoilage.

Speedy Salads

Use these time-saving tips to get supper on the table fast.

* Grill or bake extra chicken breasts, and freeze them for later use.

* Keep a can of tuna or salmon (packed in water) in your pantry for a healthful main course salad.

* Chop and freeze baked ham to have on hand.

* Chop raw vegetables for salads, and store them separately in self-sealing plastic bags. Chill up to 2 to 3 days.

Salad Mix Ins

Yield: 2 ½ cups

2	cups old-fashioned oats
1/2	cup unsalted butter, melted
1/3	cup grated Parmesan cheese
1/3	cup wheat germ
1	teaspoon dried oregano
1/2	teaspoon dried thyme
1/2	teaspoon garlic granules
1/2	teaspoon seasoned salt

1. Preheat oven to 350 degrees.

2. In a medium bowl, combine all ingredients and mix well.

3. Spread into a 15x10x1 baking pan. (Line with foil or parchment paper for easy clean-up.)

4. Bake for 15-18 minutes or until lightly browned.

5. Cool in pan on wire rack. Store in an airtight container in the refrigerator for up to 3 months.

Matching Dressings and Salad Greens

Always use a mixture of different kinds of lettuces in salads. This will ensure a variety of textures and tastes.

Dressing

Vinaigrette dressing made with olive oil and red wine vinegar.

Greens

Any greens—iceberg, romaine, leaf lettuce, butterhead lettuce, escarole, curly endive, Belgian endive, radicchio, delicate lettuces, sorrel, arugula.

Dressing

Vinaigrette dressing made with a nut oil and balsamic vinegar.

Greens

Delicate greens—butterhead lettuce, Bibb lettuce, Belgian endive, radicchio, mesclun (baby lettuces), arugula, watercress.

Dressing

Mayonnaise-based dressing such as blue cheese, green goddess, or ranch.

Greens

Hardy greens—iceberg, romaine, leaf lettuce, escarole, or curly endive.

Buttermilk Ranch Dressing

Yield: 1 cup

1/2	cup mayonnaise
3/4	cup buttermilk
1/2	tablespoon dried onion flakes
1/2	teaspoon garlic powder
1/2	teaspoon dried parsley
1/2	teaspoon dried thyme
1/8	teaspoon each, salt and white pepper

1. In a small bowl, combine ingredients thoroughly.

2. Refrigerate in a container with a lid.

Cook's note:

For a ranch dip, use sour cream or yogurt in place of buttermilk. Must be made ahead of time so the flavors can blend.

Balsamic Vinegar

For recommendations on balsamic vinegar, cooksillustrated.com recommends three brands:

Colavita—available in supermarkets nationwide.

Fini—available in specialty food stores (my favorite).

Cavalli—available in specialty food stores.

Anatomy of the Vinaigrette

Vinaigrette is a mixture of oil and vinegar seasoned with salt and pepper. The standard ratio is 3 parts oil to 1 part vinegar, but the ratio can vary. When using strong-flavored oils, less than 3 parts oil to 1 part vinegar generally will do. Citrus can be substituted for part or all of the vinegar in most recipes.

Olive oil goes well with red wine vinegar.

Nut oils go well with balsamic or sherry vinegars.

Neutral-flavored oils like canola, corn, or safflower can be mixed with flavored vinegar.

Herbs, spices, shallots, garlic, mustard, and sugar are only a few of the many flavoring ingredients used to enhance a vinaigrette dressing. If you are using dried herbs, the dressing should rest for at least 30 minutes at room temperature to allow the flavors to develop.

Basic Preparation

1. Choose an oil and vinegar that will complement each other, as well as the greens they will dress.

2. Combine the vinegar, seasonings, and any other flavorings in a bowl.

3. Whisk while adding the oil in a slow, steady stream. Continue whisking until all of the oil is incorporated.

4. To allow the flavors to blend, let the finished dressing rest for thirty minutes at room temperature.

5. Whisk immediately before use.

Variations of Vinaigrettes

Orange Vinaigrette

Use equal parts sherry and balsamic vinegar. Add 1 tablespoon orange-flavored liqueur, 2 tablespoons fresh orange juice, and 1 tablespoon minced fresh thyme. Use light olive oil.

Berry Vinaigrette

Use blueberry, strawberry, or raspberry-flavored vinegar. Add a pinch of ground cinnamon and 1/4 cup crushed fresh or frozen berries (same as the flavor of the vinegar). Use canola oil. Blend in food processor or blender.

Cheese Vinaigrette

Make a simple vinaigrette, then stir in 3 tablespoons crumbled blue cheese, goat cheese, or freshly grated Parmesan cheese.

Mustard Vinaigrette

Use balsamic vinegar, wine vinegar, or fresh lemon juice. Add 1 tablespoon Dijon mustard and 2 cloves garlic, crushed. Include 1/2 teaspoon sugar. Use extra virgin olive oil.

Curried Vinaigrette

Use fresh lemon juice. Add 1 teaspoon freshly grated ginger, 1 clove garlic, minced, 1 teaspoon curry powder, and 1/2 teaspoon dry mustard. Use sesame oil, not the toasted variety.

Caramel Pecan Sauce

Yield: 1⅔ cups

1	cup firmly packed light brown sugar
1/2	cup whipping cream
1/4	cup light corn syrup
2	tablespoons unsalted butter
1/2	cup chopped pecans
1/2	teaspoon vanilla extract

1. In a medium saucepan, combine all ingredients except vanilla extract.

2. Bring to a boil over medium heat, stirring occasionally. Boil 3–4 minutes, stirring occasionally.

3. Remove from heat, and stir in vanilla extract.

4. Cool slightly to thicken. Serve warm, and store remaining sauce in the refrigerator.

Serving style:

Place ice cream, cake, or berries in a parfait glass, margarita glass, or wine goblet. Pour sauces over, and top with whipped cream and nuts.

Cook's note:

Add these super sauces to store-bought items like:

* ❀ *High-quality ice cream*
* ❀ *Sliced angel food cake*
* ❀ *Sliced pound cake*
* ❀ *Fresh strawberries*

Hot Fudge Sauce

Yield: 1 ¼ cups

3   ounces semisweet chocolate, cut into pieces

2/3   cup sugar

      dash salt

2/3   cup evaporated milk

1. In a small saucepan, melt chocolate over very low heat, stirring constantly. Stir in sugar and salt.

2. Gradually add evaporated milk, stirring constantly. Continue to stir until mixture thickens and is hot. Serve warm, and store remaining sauce in the refrigerator.

Cook's note:

*Use a high-quality chocolate. For testing purposes in this recipe, **Ghirardelli** semisweet chocolate was used.*

Tabletop Vegetable Vase

Dinner guests can't help but smile when you display a bright bouquet in this whimsical vase surrounded by fresh asparagus spears.

Supplies

clean, empty aluminum can

rubber band

ribbon

fresh asparagus spears (about 1 ½ pounds)

1. Trim the asparagus so spears measure an inch taller than the height of the can (a large fruit cocktail or baked bean can works well for this project).

2. Place a thick rubber band around the middle of the can. Rotate the can as you add spears until the can is completely hidden. (You will use about thirty spears.)

3. Conceal the rubber band with a length of attractive ribbon that coordinates with your table decorations. Try using a 2-inch ribbon with wire edges to make it easy to shape the bow.

4. Place the vase on a round dish to prevent the cut ends of asparagus from discoloring the tablecloth or finish.

5. To complete this sunny centerpiece, fill the vase with water and your favorite fresh flowers.

Parties with Panache

- **Think green.** Plants, tablecloths, flatware, dishes, and stemware turn your tabletop into a monochromatic theme of green to welcome spring in style.

- **Daisy crazy.** Colorful daisies in galvanized buckets say, "Welcome Spring!" in fresh fashion. Change the water periodically, and the flowers can last for weeks.

- **Flower power.** Go to the fabric shop, and purchase several remnants with a beautiful floral design. To bring the "garden" inside, use the fabric as tablecloths and napkins.

- **Bowl bash.** Fill several large, clear, glass bowls with one of your favorite fruits, such as green apples, yellow lemons, and sunny oranges. This adds a splash of color and looks lovely for a centerpiece.

- **Terra-cotta time.** Use clean, napkin-lined, terra-cotta pots as serving dishes. Fill with chips, breads, silverware, or whole fruits. Give a pot containing a packet of floral or herb seeds to your friends as they leave the party.

- **Citrus centerpiece.** Fill a clear, glass cylinder with fresh lemons and limes. Insert flowers, and then tie a bow around the center of the cylinder.

Brunch for a Bunch

Menu

Vegetable and Bacon Frittata

Scrambled Egg Muffins

Apple Oatmeal Breakfast Cookies

Peach Smoothies

Probably one of the most private things in the world
is an egg, until it is broken.

—MFK Fisher

Brunch is my favorite meal. Not too early, not too late, brunch is a relaxed time, just right for enjoying family and friends. The preparation can usually be completed ahead of time. The mood is unrushed, and the food is savory—scrumptious!

Wine Time

Drinks for brunch should be lighthearted and lightly alcoholic. Consider mimosas. Mix an inexpensive sparkling wine (Freixenet) with orange juice or orange/pineapple juice—or make your favorite Bloody Mary recipe. Chill a California white (Fetzer), a German Riesling (Chateau Ste. Michelle Eroica), or a Chenin Blanc (Dry Creek or Pine Ridge) to serve with brunch.

Peach Smoothies

Cool and refreshing! Citrus and peaches are the perfect match for a smooth combination. Make ahead and set in the freezer for an icy chill.

Serves 6

1 ¼	cups milk (lowfat is OK)
1	8-ounce container lemon yogurt
1	cup orange juice
3	tablespoons sugar
1/2	teaspoon vanilla extract
1	16-ounce package frozen unsweetened peach slices

1. In a blender or food processor, combine all of the ingredients.

2. Process until blended and smooth. Serve immediately.

Variation:

Substitute peaches with raspberries or blueberries.

Apple Oatmeal Breakfast Cookies

Cookies for breakfast? You bet! These apples and oats make a healthy—yet tasty—breakfast combo.

Yield: 10

3/4	cup unsalted butter, softened
3/4	cup packed light brown sugar
2	large eggs
1	teaspoon vanilla extract
2 ½	cups old-fashioned oats
3/4	cup all-purpose flour
1/2	cup instant nonfat dry milk powder
1	teaspoon salt
1/2	teaspoon baking powder
1/2	teaspoon ground cinnamon
1 ¼	cups canned apple pie filling

1. Preheat oven to 350 degrees.

2. In a large bowl, beat the butter and brown sugar until light in color and well combined.

3. Add eggs and vanilla. Beat until incorporated.

4. In a medium bowl, combine dry ingredients. Add to the sugar and butter mixture. Mix well to combine.

5. Line two baking sheets with parchment paper. (If you do not use parchment paper, lightly grease the baking sheets.)

6. Drop by 1/4 cupfuls, 6 inches apart, onto prepared baking sheets. Lightly flour your hands, and flatten the dough into 3-inch circles.

7. Make a slight indention in the center of each circle. Top with a heaping tablespoon of pie filling.

8. Bake for 15–20 minutes, or until the edges are lightly browned. Cool 5 minutes. Remove to wire racks to cool completely.

Vegetable and Canadian Bacon Frittata

A frittata's definitive style takes breakfast meats and eggs to a higher level. Frittatas are essentially open-faced omelets of Spanish-Italian heritage. This hearty egg dish is simple to prepare and is suitable for any meal.

Serves 6–8

1	tablespoon butter
1	cup small broccoli florets
3/4	cup fresh mushrooms, sliced
2	green onions, finely chopped
1/2	cup Canadian bacon, diced
10	large eggs
1/3	cup milk
3	tablespoons Dijon mustard
3/4	teaspoon Italian seasoning
1/4	teaspoon garlic powder
1/4	teaspoon salt
1/4	teaspoon fresh ground pepper
1	Roma tomato, diced (about 1/3 cup)
1/2	cup Fontina cheese, diced into small cubes

1. Preheat oven to 375 degrees.

2. In a small skillet, over medium-low heat, melt the butter. Sauté the broccoli, mushrooms, onions, and Canadian bacon until the vegetables are tender— about 3 minutes. Remove the mixture from heat, and set it aside.

3. In a large bowl, beat eggs, milk, mustard, Italian seasonings, garlic powder, salt, and pepper until foamy.

4. Stir in tomatoes, vegetable mixture, and cubed cheese.

5. Pour into a greased, shallow 2-quart baking dish (8x11x2).

5. Bake for 25–28 minutes, or until a knife inserted near the center comes out clean.

Scrambled Egg Muffins

Savory muffins offer a unique spin on traditional breakfast sausage. Mix and match your own favorite vegetables or meats to tailor-make your muffins.

Yield: 12

1/2   pound bulk pork sausage (*Jimmy Dean Premium Original*)

12   large eggs

1/2   cup onion, chopped

1/4   cup bell pepper, seeded and chopped

1/2   teaspoon salt

1/4   teaspoon fresh ground pepper

1/4   teaspoon garlic powder

1/2   cup sharp cheddar cheese, shredded

1. Preheat oven to 350 degrees.

2. Grease a 12-cup muffin pan and set aside.

3. In a medium nonstick skillet, over medium-high heat, brown the sausage and drain.

4. In a large bowl, beat eggs, and stir in the remaining ingredients.

5. Spoon 1/3 cup of the egg mixture into each muffin cup.

6. Bake for 20–25 minutes, or until a knife inserted near the center comes out clean.

Cook's note:

You can substitute 1 cup cooked, crumbled bacon for the sausage, or you may choose to use no meat at all.

Egg-cellent Facts

Eggs are diverse. They can be eaten poached, fried, scrambled, or hard-cooked, or they can be added to batters, custards, and sauces. Luckily, this versatile food is also one of the most nutritious.

❀ **Keeping eggs fresh.** Always keep eggs in their original carton, not in the special compartment inside the refrigerator door. The carton will help prevent the delicate, porous shells from cracking and absorbing odors.

❀ **Buying.** Check the grade and sell-by date. Look inside to make sure the eggs are clean and free of cracks (wiggle them see if they stick to the carton, a sign of cracks on the bottom).

❀ **Storing.** Eggs are highly perishable and should always be refrigerated. Store the carton in the main part of the refrigerator away from the vents. Eggs are freshest within a week of purchase, but will keep for longer (about three weeks).

❀ **Judging freshness.** Chances are you'll never see a rotten egg, but if you're wondering if an egg is safe to eat, try this test: gently drop the egg in a glass of water. If it stays on the bottom or hovers in the middle, it's still fresh. If it floats to the top, it may be spoiled.

Egg-cellent Facts

* **Coloring.** The breed of the hen determines shell color. It has nothing to do with flavor or nutritional value.

* **Grading eggs.** Grading is based on quality, not size, of the egg. Grade AA are the freshest with the firmest yolks. Most supermarkets carry only grades AA and A.

* **Sizing eggs.** Eggs come in six standard sizes, classified by the minimum net ounces per dozen. When buying eggs for a specific recipe, be sure to select the size that is called for (large is the most commonly used in recipes, including those in this book). Size is especially important when baking.

* **Cooking with whites or yokes.** If a recipe calls for only yolks or whites (or different amount of each), save the leftovers. Whites can be refrigerated in an airtight container for up to four days or frozen up to twelve months. Thaw overnight in the refrigerator. Yolks should be covered with cool water. Refrigerate up to four days, and drain before using. One tablespoon of yolks equals 1 large egg yolk. Two tablespoons of whites equals 1 large egg.

* **Using other egg products.** Pasteurized liquid eggs and egg whites are made from real eggs and have been heated to kill any bacteria. Liquid egg substitutes are a blend of egg whites and other ingredients. Look for any of these in the diary case or freezer section.

* **Hard-cooking eggs**. (See page 174 for tips on hard-cooked eggs.)

Setting Up a Buffet Table

Always set up your buffet table well before your guests arrive. Plan what serving platters, bowls, and utensils you'll need for each dish, and arrange them on the table. There are many ways to help your buffet run smoothly.

❋ Don't create a buffet table "traffic jam" by serving everything on one big platter. The proceedings will run more smoothly if you spread foods out and divide them into smaller containers. It's also important that all food be presliced so it can be served quickly. This includes breads, rolls, meats, cakes, and pies—or whatever else you are serving.

❋ For convenience, group all condiments in one area. To enhance the buffet presentation, place each condiment in a small, decorative bowl with an appropriate serving utensil. Try putting the filled bowls on a lazy Susan or an interesting tray to set them apart from the main dishes.

❋ It is helpful to make small cards to identify the various dishes. This is particularly important for guests with food allergies.

❋ Wrap dining utensils in napkins, and place them in an interesting container at the end of the buffet line (consider using a mesh treasure trunk or a colorful planter). Look around your home for unusual and interesting containers with different textures and finishes. This will add a spark to your conversations, and it will make it easier for your guests to quickly grab what they need.

❋ Vary the height of your buffet table by using different sizes of small boxes or baking pans covered in fabric to match your color theme. Put your serving bowls on top of the boxes or pans. Place trays of breads or cheeses in front of the boxes or pans. This setup makes your table look full and abundant—a welcoming treat for any guest.

Decorative Tabletops

Tabletops are where your creativity can flow. Think outside the box for the most interesting designs. Setting the scene visually will make your guests feel extra special.

❉ For a quick and easy brunch or breakfast centerpiece, take a muffin pan, fill each muffin cup half-full of coffee beans, then nestle a small votive candle in each. So simple!

❉ No time to spend folding napkins? Simply pull each napkin through the hole of a small bagel, and then set one on each plate.

❉ Tiny berry baskets filled with fresh fruit look charming at each place setting. Stick a toothpick through a place card and prop it up inside. As your guests leave, give them the berry baskets as favors.

❉ Fill a large, clear bowl with fresh lemons. Use the remaining lemons as place cards. Slice one pointed side of the lemon off so it will stand up. Cut off the other side, hollow out the lemon, and place a white votive candle inside. Write each guest's name on the outside of the lemon, and place it at the top of each place setting.

May

Picnic Parade

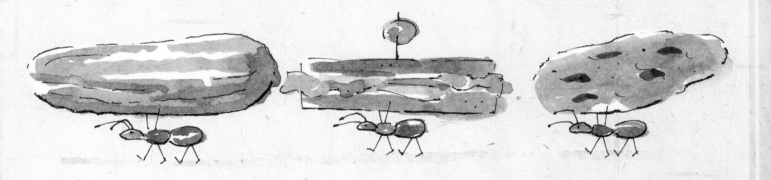

Menu

Pressed Italian Panini

Picnic Basket Baguettes

Parsley Pesto Bow Tie Salad

Watermelon-Cucumber Salad

Cookies the Way You Want
'Em When You Want 'Em

Homemade Lemonade

In France, cooking is a serious art form and a national sport.

—Julia Child

The full bloom of spring and the laziness of summer call for a delightful picnic in the park, by the lake, or in the mountains. A wicker basket lined with a colorful tablecloth and packed full of tasty treats makes this all-American experience a favorite. Picnics offer a rare opportunity to enjoy some good old-fashioned fun without the interruptions of television, laundry, or e-mail. Gather your lawn chairs, sunscreen, and bug spray, and get ready to enjoy some alfresco dining.

Wine Time

The perfect wine for a picnic is lighthearted, merry, and inexpensive. If you prefer red wine, consider Beaujolais-Villages (Georges Duboeuf), lightly chilled, or a soft and easy-on-the-palate Merlot (Geyser Peak). Look for inexpensive Merlots from Chile (Viña Casa Silva, Angostura Gran Reserva). If white wines are more your style, think about a chilled Sauvignon Blanc from New Zealand (Goldwater New Dog—this wine is sealed with a screw cap, which is becoming more and more common). For a white with a hint of sweetness, look for a Vouvray (Marc Bredif) from the French Loire region or a Viognier (Jewel) or Riesling from California (Trefethen).

Pressed Italian Panini

The flavors marry deliciously when this hearty sandwich is weighted and chilled in the refrigerator for a couple of hours before serving. To weight, place a heavy saucepan or skillet on top of the sandwich. Fill the pan with unopened canned goods, a brick wrapped in foil, or even water!

For a delicious variation, spread the cut sides of focaccia with Basil Pesto (see page 134) instead of vinaigrette.

Serves 4–6

1	8-inch round loaf Italian bread
2	cups mixed spring greens, arugula, or chopped romaine
4	ounces provolone cheese, thinly sliced
4	ounces ham, thinly sliced (or use spicy Italian capicollo)
4	ounces thinly sliced salami (or use Italian sopressata)

Vinaigrette

1/2	cup extra virgin olive oil
1/3	cup red wine vinegar
2	cloves garlic, crushed
1/2	teaspoon black pepper
1/4	teaspoon dried oregano
1/4	teaspoon salt
1/4	teaspoon crushed red pepper flakes

1. Slice bread in half horizontally, and remove some of the interior dough (save interior bread for making croutons—see page 101). Set bread aside.

2. In a small bowl, whisk together the vinaigrette ingredients. Drizzle on both sides of the cut bread.

3. Layer the greens on the bottom of the sandwich, then place the meats and cheese over the greens. End with placing the top of the sandwich over the layers.

4. Wrap tightly and place under a heavy weight in the refrigerator for 2 hours to overnight.

Picnic Basket Baguettes

You'll never miss the meat in these crunchy vegetable-and-cheese filled loaves. Slice this baguette into 2-inch servings, and arrange them on a platter with the pressed Italian panini.

Serves 4

1	6 ½-ounce container garlic-herb spreadable cheese, such as *Alouette*
1	tablespoon Dijon mustard
1/4	teaspoon garlic pepper
1	8-ounce baguette or sourdough loaf, split horizontally
6–8	thin slices baby Swiss cheese
1	7-ounce jar roasted sweet peppers, drained (to make your own, see note on page 133)
1	cup carrot, shredded
1	cup thinly sliced cucumber (seeded, if desired; see page 137)
1 ½	cups baby spinach leaves

1. In a small bowl, Stir together herbed cheese, mustard, and garlic pepper. Spread on cut sides of bread.

2. On bottom half of sandwich, layer Swiss cheese, roasted peppers, carrots, cucumber, and spinach.

3. Cover with top of loaf. Wrap tightly in plastic wrap and foil (or put in long plastic bag). Squeeze out air. Chill until serving, up to 6 hours. Slice to serve.

Roasting Sweet Bell Peppers

Cut peppers (red, yellow, or green) in half. Remove core and seeds. Place cut-side down on baking sheet. Put under oven broiler until skin is blackened and blistered, about 10 minutes. Place pepper halves in a paper bag, roll top down to close, and let sit 10 minutes. Remove from bag. Rub off and discard charred skin. Use as desired for an antipasto platter, to add to a salad, toss into pasta, tuck into sandwiches, drizzle with vinaigrette and top with feta cheese for a quick lunch with French bread. Keep covered in refrigerator for up to five days, or chop, place in jar, completely cover with olive oil, and keep in refrigerator for up to two weeks.

Toasting or Roasting Nuts

Toasting or roasting nuts reveals a new dimension of flavor, which is delicious for many dishes, but especially when using nuts as a garnish. Toasting nuts on the stove-top or roasting them in the oven will give similar results. The choice is up to you. If the oven is already on or you're roasting a large quantity, use the oven. If you need less than a cup, toasting in a skillet on the stove-top is fine. Watch nuts carefully to be sure they don't turn too brown or burn, as they'll have a bitter flavor, and you'll have to start over. When in doubt, err on the side of under-toasting or -roasting, as nuts will continue to roast even when removed from heat source.

To toast: Place nuts (chopped or whole) in a skillet and cook, stirring frequently, over medium-high heat until they are slightly darkened and give off a pleasant, toasted aroma—about 2–4 minutes. Remove from skillet immediately, as nuts will continue to toast from residual heat. Spread the nuts in a single layer on a plate to cool.

To roast: Place nuts (chopped or whole) in a single layer in a shallow baking pan or an aluminum pie pan. Roast in a medium-hot oven (350–400 degrees), watching carefully and shaking the pan periodically to roast evenly, until nuts begin to deepen in color and give off a pleasant, roasted aroma—about 5–10 minutes.

To chop: Spread nuts in a single layer on a cutting board. If using a food processor fitted with a metal blade, add nuts and use a few rapid pulses to chop them to the desired consistency. Repeat with batches of the remaining nuts. Be careful not to process the nuts too long or their oils will be released, and the nuts will turn into a paste.

Basil Pesto

Almost everyone loves this classic pesto tossed with hot pasta. It's also delicious stirred into mashed potatoes or spread on a baguette and topped with cold cuts and sliced tomatoes (see Pressed Italian Panini, page 131). Or add to a pasta salad!

Yes, you can purchase ready-made pesto. But once you see how easily this garlicky yet doable delight comes together—and you taste it—you'll opt often for whipping some up in the food processor. Pesto will keep in a tightly covered jar in the refrigerator for several weeks. For longer storage, freeze 2-tablespoon portions in an ice cube tray wrapped in plastic wrap. But it's so effortless to whip up this pesto that you'll be able to make it on a whim.

Yield: 1 cup

3	cups fresh basil leaves, rinsed and patted dry
1/4	cup pine nuts, toasted
2	cloves garlic
1	teaspoon lemon juice
1	teaspoon freshly ground black pepper
1/2	teaspoon salt
1/2	cup extra virgin olive oil
1/2	cup grated Parmesan cheese

1. Place basil, nuts, garlic, lemon juice, salt, and pepper in the bowl of food processor. Process until almost smooth. Add oil and blend thoroughly. Stir in cheese.

2. Use immediately, or place in a jar with a tight-fitting lid and refrigerate.

Parsley Pesto

Fresh in flavor, this pesto is one you can use just about anywhere. Make a "shortcut tabbouleh" by stirring this recipe into bulgur with some extra lemon juice. Tuck parsley pesto under the skin of chicken breasts before roasting. Stir some into mayonnaise to top grilled salmon, or swirl some into a serving of Cool 'n' Creamy Cucumber Soup (page 189) or any other creamy, cold soup. If you can find Italian (flat leaf) parsley, use it here; otherwise, the curly leaf variety is fine. It's milder in flavor than the flat leaf variety.

Yield: 1 cup

3	cups fresh Italian (flat leaf) parsley
1	teaspoon red wine vinegar
3	tablespoons toasted almonds, coarsely chopped
1	clove garlic
1/2	teaspoon salt
1/3	cup extra virgin olive oil
1/2	cup Romano cheese, grated

1. Place parsley, almonds, garlic, salt, and vinegar in the bowl of food processor. Process until almost smooth. Add oil. Blend. Stir in cheese.

2. Use immediately, or place in a small jar with a tight-fitting lid and refrigerate.

Parsley Pesto Bow Tie Salad

Bright green and full of flavor, this pasta salad is a fresh update on standard pasta salad. Add shredded chicken from the rotisserie to turn this into a main dish. This salad is best if served at room temperature the day it's made.

Serves 6–8

12	ounces farfalle (bow tie) pasta, cooked in boiling, salted water and drained
2	tablespoons red wine vinegar
1/2	teaspoon crushed red pepper flakes
1	cup Parsley Pesto
1/2	cup (4 ounces) feta cheese, crumbled

1. In a large bowl, place pasta.
2. Toss with vinegar and crushed red pepper.
3. Add pesto, and toss well to coat the pasta.

Watermelon-Cucumber Salad

What a surprise—watermelon as a spicy, savory, and sweet salad! This colorful mixture makes a refreshing salad for a picnic. For the Fourth of July, add a pint of blueberries for a red-white-and-blue side dish anyone would be proud of. Look for the smaller-sized watermelons widely available today.

This salad is best served the day it is made.

Yield: 12 cups

1/4	cup distilled white vinegar
1/4	cup sugar
1/4	teaspoon crushed red pepper flakes
4	cucumbers, peeled, halved, and seeded
8	cups cubed, seeded watermelon (from a 3-pound piece of watermelon)
1/2	cup fresh mint leaves, chopped

1. In a small saucepan, boil vinegar, sugar, and pepper, stirring to dissolve sugar. Remove from heat. Chill syrup in refrigerator while preparing cucumber and watermelon.

2. In large bowl, gently toss cucumber, watermelon, syrup, and mint. Taste, and add more crushed red pepper flakes if desired.

Cucumber Capers

To peel and seed cucumbers, peel cucumbers with a swivel-type peeler or carefully with a paring knife. Cut in half lengthwise. With a small spoon, scrape out the seeds and discard them.

Homemade Lemonade

Lemons at room temperature will yield more juice than chilled ones. To get the most juice from a fresh lemon, roll it back and forth under your palm on a hard surface to gently "break" some of the juice cells under the lemon skin. You'll get about 1 cup of juice from six small lemons or four large ones.

Yield: 1/2 gallon

4	cups water, divided
1	cup sugar
3	cups ice
1	cup fresh lemon juice (or use one 7 ½-ounce container frozen fresh lemon juice, such as *Minute Maid*, thawed)

1. In a small sauce pan, boil 1 cup of water and the sugar, stirring to dissolve sugar. Remove from heat. Chill in refrigerator until cool.

2. Put ice in a half-gallon container. Stir in syrup, lemon juice, and the remaining 3 cups water.

Lemonade Stand

Variations on Homemade Lemonade

Mint Lemonade: Add a handful of fresh mint leaves when making the sugar syrup. Strain syrup into a container, discarding mint. Proceed as directed for homemade lemonade.

Peach Lemonade: Add four peach tea bags when making sugar syrup. Strain syrup into container, discarding tea bags. Proceed as directed for homemade lemonade, adding 3/4 cup peach nectar with the lemon juice and 3 cups of water.

Watermelon Lemonade: Blend 8 cups cubed, seeded watermelon in a food processor or blender until puréed. Proceed as directed, straining watermelon purée into container in place of the 3 cups of water.

Sparkling Ginger Lemonade: Add 6 tablespoons peeled, minced ginger root when making sugar syrup. Strain syrup into container, discarding ginger. Proceed as directed, adding 3 cups chilled ginger ale in place of the 3 cups water.

Raspberry Lemonade: Blend one 10-ounce package frozen raspberries (in syrup) in a blender or food processor. Strain seeds out. Proceed as directed, adding raspberries with the lemon juice and 3 cups of water.

Pineapple Lemonade: Proceed as directed, adding 3 cups chilled pineapple juice in place of the 3 cups of water.

Cookies the Way You Want 'Em When You Want 'Em

Who doesn't love a just-baked cookie? No one I know. But who knew you could have a homemade, warm-from-the-oven cookie whenever you wanted? This cookie dough is made when you have time, and is then frozen into cookie-sized portions to take from the freezer to the oven whenever you're in the mood.

This recipe is a good excuse to invest in a 2-ounce scoop. Your cookies will be uniform in size if you use a scoop measure, and you'll find lots of other uses for it, too—such as making melon balls or scooping sherbet.

Yield: 2 ½ dozen

1	cup unsalted butter (2 sticks)
3/4	cup sugar
3/4	cup packed light brown sugar
2	teaspoons vanilla extract
2	large eggs
3	cups all-purpose flour
1	teaspoon salt
1	teaspoon baking powder
1/2	teaspoon baking soda

Cook's note:

You may add additional ingredients as desired (see add-ins on page 141).

1. Preheat oven to 375 degrees.

2. Using an electric mixer, beat butter and sugars together until well combined and just light in color. (If you overmix, the cookies will spread out too much on the baking sheet.) Add vanilla and eggs, and beat until thoroughly combined.

3. In a medium bowl, combine flour, salt, baking powder, and baking soda. Beat into creamed mixture.

4. Drop dough from a 2-ounce (2 tablespoons or 1/8 cup) scoop about 1 ½ inches apart onto ungreased cookie sheets. Bake 14–16 minutes, or until edges just begin to brown. Remove to rack to cool.

Flour Power

Instead of dipping the dry measuring cup into the flour, spoon the flour into the cup, then level it with the straight edge of a knife.

Add-in: Extracts in addition to (not in place of) vanilla. Try 1 teaspoon rum, peppermint, lemon, or almond. Add with eggs.

Add-in: Spices. Add 1/2 teaspoon nutmeg or ginger, or 1 teaspoon cinnamon. Add with dry ingredients.

Add-in: 1 to 1 ½ cups of different-flavored chips (chocolate, butterscotch, peanut butter, mint, or toffee), chopped nuts (pecans, almonds, or walnuts), dried fruit, chopped if necessary (currants, raisins, apricots, or dates), shredded coconut, or oatmeal. Stir in after adding dry ingredients.

Cook's notes:

Use parchment paper to line cookie sheets for easier cleanup. Let cookie sheets cool before reloading to bake. (Parchment paper is found in the supermarket with the foil and wax paper.)

Bake as many cookies as you want today. Portion the rest onto a cookie sheet, and freeze uncovered for at least 30 minutes. Remove cookie dough balls to a freezer self-sealing freezer bag.

Baking frozen dough: When ready to bake, remove frozen dough balls from freezer, place on cookie sheets, and bake in 375-degree oven for 14–16 minutes.

High-altitude adjustments: above 4,000 feet, use 1/2 teaspoon baking powder and 1/4 teaspoon baking soda.

Baking Sheet Repeat

Baking batch after batch of cookies can be a frustrating exercise, especially when you have only one cookie sheet. No one wants to scrub the same baking sheet many times, but dough balls must be placed on a clean surface. Here's how to work quickly and efficiently when you have just one cookie sheet.

1. Load a sheet of parchment paper with balls of dough. Slide the paper onto the cookie sheet, and place cookies in the oven.

2. While the first batch is baking, load a second piece of parchment paper with balls of dough.

3. When the baked cookies come out of the oven, whisk the dough ball-loaded parchment paper onto a cooling rack. After cooling the baking sheet with a quick, cool water rinse and dry, it's ready for the next batch, which has already been prepared!

Picnic Pointers

To safely transport foods to a picnic, remember these toting hints.

✤ The bacteria that cause food-borne illnesses thrive at temperatures between 41 and 135 degrees, so don't leave prepared foods unrefrigerated for more than 2 hours. If the temperature is over 90 degrees, the time limit should be shortened to 1 hour. Discard any leftovers.

✤ Don't pack chilled foods in insulated coolers until just before you leave home. Surround the foods with plenty of ice or ice packs. Use two coolers—one for drinks and the other for perishable foods. This way, warm air won't reach the foods each time someone grabs a beverage.

✤ When the weather is hot, transport the coolers in the air-conditioned, passenger compartment of the car, not in the hot trunk. Once at the picnic site, keep the coolers in the shade.

✤ Wash your hands before and after handling food. Soap and hot water are ideal, but a jug of water and soap will do in a pinch. Disposable moist towelettes are a good option, too.

Picnic Basket Packing List

Prevent picnic pitfalls by reviewing this list of items you may want to bring along as you grab your picnic basket and head out the door:

* Tablecloth or blanket

* Floor pillows or beach chairs

* Plates

* Cups

* Flatware

* Napkins

* Serving utensils

* Salt and pepper

* Condiments

* Paring knife

* Cutting board

* Bottle opener

* Paper towels or moistened hand wipes

* Plastic bags for dirty dishes

* Garbage bags and twist ties

* Insect repellent

* Sunscreen

* Charcoal and lighter fluid

* Matches

Ambience on the Quilt

All picnics are not created equal, and a meal outside does not a party make if the food isn't right, the bugs are biting, and you leave the corkscrew in the car after hiking like a pack mule up a hill. A little bit of forethought will make a huge difference.

Making a checklist is standard operating procedure for caterers and is a great habit to develop when packing food items to eat away from home.

* Make a list of all the food, drinks, and necessary serving utensils and containers.

* Take a blanket or a large-sized quilt. Don't forget floor pillows or beach chairs for lounging.

* No one can be comfortable with mosquitoes or horseflies buzzing about. Citronella candles and insect repellent are worthy additions to the picnic tote.

* Scout the location in advance, and determine exactly where you want to set up your picnic. An area with shade is imperative.

* Sunscreen and umbrellas are desirable for adults but mandatory for small children and babies. If you don't already have one in your car, buy a small first-aid kit for skinned knees and bug bites.

* Place a group of small stones in the corners of the tablecloth. Pull the corners up around the stones, and tie with a ribbon. This will help anchor your cloth if it is a windy day.

* There's no reason to disregard the need for proper tableware outdoors. Look for reusable, lightweight, and durable plastic plates, knives, forks, and spoons. Reusable sets are better for the environment, and they make a more attractive table.

* When preparing meals for picnics at a concert, bite-sized things are best. However tasty, no one wants to wind up with a slab of perfectly seasoned, grilled eggplant in his or her lap.

* Don't forget food safety. Group the cold foods together, and wrap them in newspaper to insulate.

* Coolers are undoubtedly best for keeping food cold, but keep an eye out for lightweight, insulated tote bags with long shoulder straps. The bags are not the best for keeping food cold for a long period, but for a short time, they are far easier on the back. You might also consider purchasing a cooler on wheels.

* Pack a roll of paper towels for cleanup, and make sure to take plenty of napkins for sticky fingers. Take a container of moistened wipes for real messes.

* All that paper has to go somewhere, so be sure to bring a couple of trash bags with you so you can remove all the trash. Remember the rule: "Take only photographs and leave only footprints."

Pack Practically

Whether your outing is for two or twenty, you're sure to have a good time if you keep these picnic pointers in mind:

* Consider packing in two containers—a picnic basket for tableware and nonperishable items, and a cooler for cold food and beverages.

* To make it easy to get at the items you need when you arrive at your picnic site, pack your basket in reverse order. Place nonperishable food on the bottom, then add serving items and tableware, and finally place the tablecloth on top.

* To avoid leftovers, closely estimate how much food your group will eat. Unless it can be kept very cold or very hot, the food could spoil. It is just not a good idea to consume leftovers after picnicking.

* Bring along plastic bags to cart home dirty dishes and silverware.

Keep Your Cool

Cold sandwiches, chilled salads, and icy beverages really hit the spot on warm days. To ensure that these items stay cool and safe to eat, remember the rules.

* Cold foods should be kept at 41 degrees or colder.

* When packing a cooler, it should be about 25 percent ice and 75 percent food. Place ice packs on the bottom and along the sides of the cooler. Then place the heaviest and most perishable foods on top of the ice packs. Fill in with lighter items.

* Fill liter bottles with water and freeze. Using this instead of ice will keep your cooler cold, keep your food packages from getting wet, and provide drinking water as it melts.

* Transfer chilled foods directly from the refrigerator to the cooler. Do not use the cooler to chill warm or room-temperature items.

* A full cooler will stay cold longer than one that is partially empty, so choose an appropriate-sized cooler. If the food doesn't completely fill your cooler, add more ice.

* To protect your cooler from the sun's rays, place it in the shade as soon as you arrive at your picnic spot.

* When setting out chilled salads or other cold foods, consider placing the serving containers in a larger pan filled with ice to keep them cold.

Safe Grilling

While subs and other sandwiches are common alfresco fare, grilled foods are popular, too. If you plan to cook meals such as chicken, steak, hamburgers, or hot dogs at your picnic site, review these helpful hints:

* Wrap raw meat, poultry, or fish in airtight plastic containers or resealable plastic bags—keep separate from cooked foods.

* Freeze meats before packing so they remain cold longer. This is especially important if you must travel a long distance to the picnic location or if the foods won't be grilled immediately upon arrival.

* Do not partially cook foods at home to speed up cooking at the picnic site. Bacteria grows faster in partially cooked foods.

* Hot foods should be kept at 135 degrees or hotter and should be eaten within two hours of being cooked.

Saucing Up the Settings

Since summer is the time for outdoor entertaining, why not create place markers with items from your own backyard? Smooth pretty stones not only designate where guests sit, they also work wonderfully for holding down paper napkins when the wind begins to blow.

Using an opaque paint pen from a craft or stationery store, write the name of each dinner guest on a clean, dry stone. Feel free to include a design or small drawing, too. Once the paint dries completely, the stones are ready to be set on your table. If you're unable to find enough smooth stones, you can buy small bags of them from the floral departments of craft stores or discount retailers.

Paper Products

While cloth napkins add elegance to special occasions, paper napkins have their place at the table, too. They are especially handy for casual get-togethers like picnics or barbecues because they are disposable and are sold in numerous colors, styles, and designs. For a special touch, use paper napkins to bundle each guest's utensils. Secure the packages with coordinating ribbon, twine, freshly cut ivy, decorative cord, or raffia. Purchase fun fabric or remnants from your favorite fabric store, cut into a 12-inch square, and trim the edges with pinking shears. These serve as instant, disposable cloth napkins.

Four Ways to Beat the Heat

Outdoor eating can be stifling in the heat. Try these warm-weather tips for keeping your cool.

* Table centerpieces of fresh flowers will wilt before the grill gets going, so try a tropical arrangement of coconuts, limes, lemons, and pineapples in a large bowl or galvanized bucket.

* Washcloths frozen in a mix of water and lemon juice can be rolled up and stacked on a platter for guests' fingers after a messy meal.

* *Junior Mints* frozen on a cookie tray can be transferred to a bowl for after-dinner mints for guests.

* Beat the heat with a mid-morning picnic brunch of muffins, sweet breads, sandwiches of Brie and apple, or BLTs assembled at the picnic site with a platter of cheese and fruits.

Equipped with these tips and a packed picnic basket, you're ready to go. All that's left is choosing a place to spread out your portable feast. Consider the banks of a nearby lake or stream, a local park, or a shady spot in your own backyard. Then sit back, relax, and enjoy a picture-perfect picnic. If the weather chooses not to cooperate with your outdoor plans, move to your porch or the floor of your den.

June

Dressed to Grill

Menu

Grilled Fish Steaks
with Mango Salsa

Grilled Veggies Antipasto

Fruited Couscous Salad

Grilled Peach Melba

I don't like gourmet cooking or "this" cooking or "that" cooking. I like good cooking.

—James Beard

I love the sounds of summer—the whisper of propane gas warming up the grill, the squish of chicken marinating in a self-sealing bag, and the sizzle of a rack of ribs. 'Tis the season to be grilling! This year, why not share the joy of cooking out? Whether in an apartment or on a neighborhood street, use this opportunity to meet others and share good foods. What better way to build friendships, introduce new neighbors, and try terrific recipes? In the meantime, it wouldn't hurt to bone up on some grilling and party-throwing skills. By the time your party is in full swing, your guests will not only think you're an old pro at the grill, they'll also realize your party will go down in history as the party to which all other get-togethers are compared.

Wine Time

Some consider only beer when planning a grill menu, but wine can also be a perfect companion to grilled foods. A flavorful, spicy red wine like a Zinfandel (Rosenblum or Klein) from California may have a hint of smoke—perfect for a grill menu. Many fish steaks are hearty, pairing nicely with a red wine. If you prefer to offer a white wine, a medium-bodied Sauvignon Blanc from South Africa (Graham Beck) would complement this menu.

Grilled Veggies Antipasto

You'll return to the grill again and again to fix vegetables. The slightly smoky, charred flavor is just the twist to add fantastic flavor to your old favorites. You may serve this recipe as a casual first course, or you might think about serving it as a side dish to grilled sausage, pork tenderloin, chicken, or fish.

The veggies can be grilled a day ahead of time. To store, put each variety of veggie in a separate self-sealing bag. Add a little olive oil to each bag to lightly coat the vegetables. Seal bags, and refrigerate for up to five days.

Serves 8–10

2	medium bell peppers (red or yellow), cut in half lengthwise and seeded
1	medium eggplant, cut lengthwise into 1/2-inch slices
1	large sweet onion, sliced thickly (Vidalia or Maui)
2	medium zucchini, cut in half lengthwise
1	pound fresh asparagus spears, woody ends snapped off
6	plum tomatoes, halved lengthwise
	olive oil
	salt and freshly ground black pepper

1. Prepare a hot fire in the grill. Brush all veggies lightly with olive oil, and season with salt and pepper.

2. Grill all veggies, in batches if necessary, turning as needed until tender and charred, 10–20 minutes. Remove from grill and bring to room temperature.

3. Mound grilled veggies on a large platter. Surround with fresh mozzarella cheese, a variety of olives, breadsticks, or crusty Italian or French bread. Serve with red wine vinegar to drizzle over vegetables.

Grill Tips

Minimal preparation, quick cooking, and easy cleanup make grilling a technique worth mastering. Try these tips for success:

Preparing the Grill. Remove charred particles with a stiff brush before each use. Use a chimney starter to light the coals. Allow them to smolder until covered with white ash. If you are using a gas grill, preheat it. You can create zones of varying temperature by gathering the coals into a pile to one side of the grill. To gauge the heat level, count how long you can hold your hand one-inch above the grill—1 to 2 seconds is high heat, 3 to 5 seconds is medium, and 6 seconds or more is low.

Preparing the Food. If you're grilling more than one type of food, cook the denser foods a few minutes before starting the more tender items. Lightly coat food with oil to prevent it from sticking to the grill.

Cooking the Food. Foods with short cooking times should be grilled directly above the coals. Larger pieces require slower cooking and a longer cooking period. Place these pieces over the areas with fewer or no coals. The heat within the grill will cook the food.

Marking the First Side. Place the presentation side down on the grill. Distinct marks will char onto its surface. Cook the food undisturbed until it is ready for turning. This develops better flavor and allows the food to release naturally from the grill, without sticking or tearing. Use a spatula or tongs to avoid piercing the food and losing juices.

Lifting the Lid. Keep the lid closed to speed cooking time and reduce flare-ups. Lifting the lid lowers the temperature. "Grilling is an aggressive cooking method that can dry out foods if not done properly," warns Bruce Mattel, associate professor in culinary arts at the Culinary Institute of America. "Many items intended for grilling benefit from being marinated prior to cooking. This technique adds flavor and complexity and will also help with moisture retention."

Grilling 101

The right grilling accessories are essential for safety, and they allow you to grill mouthwatering foods with ease. Some must-haves include the following:

* Meat thermometer
* Long-handled, spring-loaded tongs
* Water spritzer (for charcoal grills)
* Fire extinguisher

* Long-handled basting brush
* Long-handled metal spatula
* Heavy-duty cooking mitt

To handle flare-ups in charcoal grills, spray water directly at coals. Gas grill manufacturers do not recommend spraying flare-ups with water. Therefore, it's important to drain excess oil or marinade before putting food on the grill. Also, trim the excess fat from steaks and chops to discourage flare-ups.

Grilled Fish Steaks with Mango Salsa

Fish steaks grill wonderfully. Just be careful not to overcook them, as even fatty fish like salmon can turn dry on the grill. Marinate briefly, and grill quickly. The mango salsa is a tropical, crowning touch for any fish from the grill. Steaks of tuna, swordfish, halibut, or salmon are good grilling candidates.

Serves 6

6	8-ounce fish steaks, cut 1-inch thick
5	tablespoons olive oil
5	tablespoons lime juice
1	teaspoon seasoned salt, such as *Lawry's*
	Mango Chili Salsa (see page 160)

1. Place fish in a shallow glass dish. Whisk together oil, lime juice, and salt, and pour over fish. Cover and let marinate for 30 minutes in the refrigerator.

2. Light a hot fire in the grill. Lift fish steaks from the marinade, reserving the marinade for basting.

3. Grill fish, basting occasionally with the marinade, turning once, until the marinade is used up and the fish flesh becomes firm when pressed with a finger and begins to flake.

4. Remove fish from grill a couple of minutes before the fish is fully cooked. The heat within the fish will finish the cooking process, leaving a juicy fish steak. Let it sit about 8–10 minutes total. Serve with Mango Chili Salsa.

Mango Chili Salsa

This sweet and savory salsa is perfect for almost any grilled fish. Its slightly tropical personality comes from mango, whose sweet profile is heightened with savory and piquant ingredients of jalapeno, lime, vinegar, and red onion. If you're looking for super heat, substitute a serrano chili for the jalapeno.

The salsa is best if made shortly before serving.

Yield: 2 cups

2	ripe mangoes, peeled and diced (see page 203)
2	tablespoons red onion, minced
1/4	cup fresh cilantro, minced
2	tablespoons fresh lime juice
2	tablespoons jalapeno chili, minced (or 1/4 to 1/2 teaspoon crushed red pepper)
1/4	teaspoon salt

In a serving bowl, toss mango, onion, cilantro, lime juice, jalapeno, and salt.

Fish Steaks

Fish steaks are pieces of fish cut perpendicular to the body from back to belly. Fish fillets, on the other hand, are pieces of fish cut along the length of the body from head to tail. Steaks generally come from large, round fish, whereas fillets come from flat fish. Fillets can be grilled, but cook them very quickly because they're generally much thinner than the crosscut steaks.

Fruited Couscous Salad

You'll find many occasions to make and serve this versatile salad made with the delicious pasta with a funny name—couscous. Couscous cooks quickly and effortlessly. Simply cover with hot water, broth, or as with this salad, juice. It's ready after 5 minutes of steaming.

Serves 6–8

2	cups orange juice
1/2	teaspoon salt
1	10-ounce package plain couscous

Dressing

1/4	cup red wine vinegar
1/4	cup olive oil
2	tablespoons honey
1	teaspoon salt
1	teaspoon ground cumin
1/2	teaspoon ground cinnamon
1/2	cup dried apricots, chopped
1/2	cup dried cranberries
1	cup baby spinach, chopped
4	tablespoons slivered almonds
1/2	cup fresh mint leaves, chopped

1. In a medium sauce pan over high heat, bring orange juice and salt to a boil. Remove from heat, stir in couscous, cover, and let stand 5 minutes.

2. Meanwhile, whisk together dressing ingredients.

3. Fluff couscous with a fork and place in serving bowl; stir in apricots, cranberries, spinach, and nuts. Pour dressing over mixture and toss gently.

Cook's notes:

Feel free to substitute or add golden raisins or currants, or even try fresh fruit—diced peaches or nectarines, if in season.

For a different flavor, substitute 1/2–1 teaspoon curry powder for the cumin and cinnamon.

To chop spinach, stack several leaves of spinach, roll like a cigar, and cut on the diagonal.

Chopping Dried Fruit

Kitchen shears are the secret tool for preparing dried fruits like apricots, peaches, or apples. Spray the shears with nonstick cooking spray. Place fruit in a measuring cup, and snip to desired-sized pieces.

Grilled Peach Melba

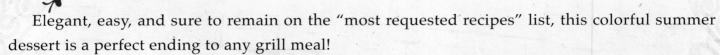

Elegant, easy, and sure to remain on the "most requested recipes" list, this colorful summer dessert is a perfect ending to any grill meal!

Before preparing this easy but impressive dessert, clean the grill. While the grill is hot, scrub well with a wire grill brush to clean and remove any particles of food.

Serves 6–8

1   10 ¾-ounce frozen pound cake, sliced 1/2-inch thick

4   large ripe peaches, halved and pitted (or 1 15 ¼-ounce can freestone peach halves, drained)

      canola oil

2   10-ounce packages frozen sweetened raspberries, thawed

      whipped heavy cream in an aerosol can (read label to be sure you are getting 100 percent cream)

1/2 cup sliced almonds, toasted

1. Slice cake into 1/2-inch slices. Toast them on a hot grill, turning once. Place toasted cake slices onto six dessert plates or in shallow dessert bowls.

2. Lightly brush peaches with canola oil, and place on grill.

3. Grill 3–4 minutes, turning once, or until the grill lightly marks the peach halves. Place each peach half onto a cake-lined plate.

4. Evenly ladle raspberries over the peaches. Garnish with whipped cream and almonds. Serve immediately.

Cook's note:

This will work in a grill pan on top of the stove. Brush the pound cake lightly with butter before grilling.

Icebreaker Intros

Create place cards beforehand. Put each attendee's name on one side, and to encourage conversation at each table, put one of the following questions on the other.

❋ Where is your favorite vacation spot?

❋ What's your fondest childhood memory?

❋ What books have you recently read?

❋ Where would you like to live if you didn't live in this city?

❋ What kind of music do you like?

❋ What's the latest movie you've seen?

❋ What's your favorite sport?

❋ What was your favorite wedding gift and why?

Parties with Panache

❋ **Go fresh.** Close to party time, buy the freshest produce and meats possible.

❋ **Have fun.** Create a party environment. Gather some old vegetable crates from your local farmer's market. Cover your back patio with plastic, and splatter-paint the crates to add some color. Use the crates as serving pieces or containers for flowerpots, or turn them upside down to create levels to your buffet. Remember, visual appeal matters.

❋ **Clean up easily and save money.** Use washable or plastic tablecloths, napkins, and chairs. Go to your favorite discount party store for festive additions to your party décor. Borrow these items from friends or family to make this bash affordable.

❋ **Don't forget the music.** If your party has a theme, play it up. If you've planned a country-western theme in your backyard, play country CDs, and decorate with cowboy boots stuffed with flowers and bandannas to boost the festive vibe. Simple swirls of rope, with a lantern or a candle in the middle, make cute centerpieces.

❋ **Display carefully.** Look around your home for interesting, tall containers to hold the silverware. A unique wooden box works nicely for holding napkins.

❋ **Decorate ice cubes.** Bright colors and different shapes add a cool splash of color and flavor to glasses of sparkling water or summer cocktails. Drop strips of fresh citrus zest into empty ice cube trays. Add water to trays and freeze. Try using berries, small grapes, or mint leaves.

Star-Spangled Supper

Menu

Barbecue Circuit-
Approved Beef Brisket

Splendid Bourbon-
Barbecued Beans

Better-Than-Mom's Potato Salad

Red, White, and Blue Slaw

All-American Cherry Pie

Don't take a butcher's advice on how to cook meat.
If he knew, he'd be a chef.

—Andy Rooney

Celebrate America in style! Red, white, and blue line the storefronts, porches, and flagpoles. Homemade vanilla ice cream topped with fresh strawberries and blueberries, potato salad chilling in the cooler, iced tea ready to drink—nothing beats nostalgic recipes when celebrating our country's freedom. This is a perfect meal to make ahead and enjoy while watching the sparkle and shine of a fabulous fireworks display.

Wine Time

A summer day of celebration might indicate a tub of iced beer for some. For wine lovers, the Fourth is a great excuse to enjoy bottles from all-American vines. For this traditional Independence Day feast, open a Fess Parker Syrah or Pinot Noir from California (Acacia). Offer a chilled White Zinfandel (Buehler from Napa Valley), and certainly consider a sparkling rosé (Gloria Ferrer or Domaine Carneros) to toast during fireworks.

Barbecue Sauce

This recipe belonged to my favorite cook—my grandmother. This sauce is a rich blend of chili, vinegar, and brown sugar, with a tangy tomato base. A real winner served with any type of meat, this prize-winning recipe won a second-place ribbon in the canning division at the State Fair of Texas.

Yield: 2 cups

1	tablespoon butter
1	onion, chopped
4	cloves garlic, minced
1	bay leaf
1/2	lemon, juiced (reserve rind)
2/3	cup chili sauce
2/3	cup Worcestershire sauce
1 ¾	cup ketchup
1/2	cup red wine vinegar
1/4	cup packed light brown sugar
1/2	teaspoon *Tabasco*

1. In a 4- to 5-quart Dutch oven, melt butter over medium heat.

2. Add onion and garlic, and sauté 5–6 minutes, or until onion is tender.

3. Stir in the remaining ingredients, including lemon rind. Bring to a boil. Reduce heat and simmer 15 minutes.

4. Pour mixture through a wire mesh strainer into a bowl, discarding the solids.

Cook's note:

Give as a gift, or refrigerate for two weeks. Can be frozen for one month.

Barbecue Circuit-Approved Beef Brisket

Plan ahead! This is an all-day affair on the grill or smoker, but it doesn't take much fuss. Slow smoking is the secret to this succulent brisket. The brisket, a tough cut favored by barbecue pit masters from El Paso to Memphis to Kansas City, melts to tenderness after wrapping it in foil (which simulates moist-heat cooking), so don't skip the final step of wrapping and returning to the grill.

Serves 8–12

1	3 ½–5-pound fresh beef brisket
	Barbecue Brisket Paste (see page 171, or use your own favorite BBQ rub)
4–6	cups hickory chips
1	cup beer or water
1	cup cider vinegar
1	tablespoon Worcestershire sauce
1/2	yellow onion, coarsely chopped
4	cloves garlic, crushed

1. Rub brisket with barbecue paste. Place in baking dish. Cover and refrigerate 6–24 hours.

2. An hour before cooking, cover hickory chips in water and soak. Prepare smoker or grill for indirect cooking. Drain hickory chips and sprinkle over hot coals, for a charcoal grill. For a gas grill, wrap soaked wood chips in aluminum foil. Punch small holes in the foil to release the smoke, and place aluminum package on the grill, directly over the heat source.

3. Place drip pan in smoker or grill. Add beer, vinegar, Worcestershire, onion, and garlic to drip pan. When the heat in the smoker or grill stabilizes at 225 degrees (use an oven thermometer placed inside the grill, close to the brisket but not directly over the heat source, to determine grill temperature), uncover the brisket, and place it on the rack over the drip pan. Cover the smoker or grill, and smoke for 4 hours, replenishing chips as needed for smoke. Plan on a handful (about 1/4 cup) of chips every hour for gas grills. When the aluminum packet of chips stops smoking, replace it.

4. Brush top of brisket every hour with drip pan juices. Smoke for a total of 6 hours.

5. Remove meat from smoker or grill. Brush again with drip-pan juice. Wrap meat in heavy foil. Return to the smoker or grill, and cook for 1–2 hours more, or until tender.

6. Let brisket rest at least 10 minutes after removing it from smoker or grill. Slice across the grain or shred to serve.

Barbecue Brisket Paste. In small bowl, stir together 2 tablespoons each: cayenne, black pepper, granulated garlic, plus 1/4 cup paprika. Stir in 2 tablespoons olive oil to make a paste. Spread on all surfaces of brisket.

Oven-Barbecued Brisket. Place brisket in a 13x9x2-inch baking pan. In a small bowl, combine 2 tablespoons liquid smoke, 2 teaspoons black pepper, 2 teaspoons Worcestershire sauce, and 1 teaspoon each granulated garlic and granulated onion. Rub the seasoning mixture on all surfaces of the brisket. Cover with foil and refrigerate overnight. Add 1/2 cup beer to baking pan. Cover brisket tightly with foil, and bake in a 325-degree oven for 4 hours. Slice across the grain or shred to serve.

While some barbecue masters turn up their noses at the thought of a sauce ruining their masterpiece from the grill, many people welcome a douse or more of barbecue sauce. The secret is to taste continually as you're making your own concoction.

Stylin' Up Your Sauce. Start with a purchased, tomato-based barbecue sauce, and go crazy!

❋ Choose an "original" style to start doctoring, remembering to taste as you add.

❋ Make a mixture of half sauce and half orange marmalade (or other jam or preserves— try plum or apricot). Add a teaspoon of hot pepper sauce, such as *Tabasco*.

❋ Stir in one tablespoon prepared horseradish for a real punch of flavor.

❋ For extra tang, stir in some cider vinegar a tablespoon at a time. Taste before saucing!

❋ Want an extra touch of smoke? Add some liquid smoke, 1/2 teaspoon at a time. Taste to make sure it fits your family's and guests' palettes.

Grilling Methods

❧ **Indirect Grilling.** Use with larger cuts of meat or poultry that would burn on the outside and not be done inside if placed over direct heat on the grill. The idea is similar to the indirect heat in an oven. Indirect grilling can be used in both covered charcoal and gas grills.

❧ **Charcoal Grill.** Build the coals on one side of the charcoal grate with a drip pan on the other side, or arrange coals in a circle around the outer edge of the charcoal grate with the drip pan in the middle.

❧ **Gas Grill.** After preheating the grill, turn off any burners directly below the food. This usually is done by putting meat on one side of the grill, and leaving the burners "ON" on the other side of the grill.

❧ **Drip Pan.** A drip pan is simply a pan (disposable aluminum works fine) placed underneath the meat on the grill. The pan catches drips from the meat and holds liquid to help keep meat moist on the grill.

Smoking Wood

Some common wood chips used for smoking:

Apple—fruity, slightly sweet.

Cedar—medium-strong flavor, sweet, piney.

Hickory—pungent, smoky, bacon-like.

Mesquite—strong, earthy flavor.

Red Oak—heavy smoke flavor.

Splendid Bourbon-Barbecued Beans

These doctored canned beans beat all! You'll add this recipe to your "most requested" list when you're planning a menu for a barbecue. They make a happy mate to burgers, ribs, pork chops, chicken, hot dogs—just about anything from the grill. For a "teetotaler's version," substitute apple juice for the bourbon.

Serves 8–10

6	slices lean bacon, sliced in 1/2-inch pieces
3/4	cup onion, diced
1/2	red bell pepper, seeded and diced
1/2	green pepper, seeded and diced
1/2	cup packed light brown sugar
2/3	cup tomato-based barbecue sauce
1/3	cup bourbon
4	tablespoons spicy brown, prepared mustard
1/3	cup maple-flavored pancake syrup
2	28-ounce cans pork and beans, drained

1. Preheat oven to 400 degrees.

2. In a large skillet over high heat, fry bacon until lightly browned. Stir in onion and peppers. Sauté for 3 minutes until vegetables are crisp-tender.

3. In a large bowl, place skillet contents along with remaining ingredients. Mix together, and then place in a 13x9-inch casserole dish.

4. Heat, covered loosely with foil, for 40–60 minutes, stirring 2 or 3 times.

How Much Does It Hold?

Not sure how much your baking pans hold? Fill with water from a measuring cup to determine. Although this recipe may make a total volume of 8 cups, you need space so beans don't overflow the baking dish.

Better-Than-Mom's Potato Salad

Shhhhh! I won't tell, and you won't brag—but the proof is in the tasting. The secret to this potato salad is letting the warm potatoes soak up flavor from the vinaigrette, and this one has sweet pickle juice added. Use the juice from a jar of sweet gherkins or bread 'n' butter pickles.

Serves 8–12

2	16-ounce packages refrigerated, diced potatoes (from the produce section)
1	8-ounce container sour cream
1/2	cup mayonnaise
1	teaspoon celery seed
3	tablespoons fresh chives
1	medium sweet onion, chopped (Vidalia or Maui)
2	stalks celery, sliced
3	hard-cooked eggs, coarsely chopped
1	cup sweet pickles, drained (reserving juice) and chopped

Vinaigrette

3	tablespoons red wine vinegar
3	tablespoons prepared yellow mustard
2	tablespoons sweet pickle juice
1	teaspoon salt
1/2	teaspoon freshly ground black pepper

1. Preheat oven to 450 degrees.

2. Spread potatoes in a shallow, greased pan, and roast them for 15 minutes.

3. In a large bowl, whisk together the vinaigrette ingredients. Add potatoes and stir to coat. Let stand 10 minutes, or until they reach room temperature.

4. Stir together sour cream, mayonnaise, celery seed, and chives. Add to potato mixture. Toss lightly to coat. Gently fold in celery, eggs, and sweet pickles. Cover and chill several hours.

Hard-Cooked Eggs

Hard-cooked eggs are also called hard-boiled. Both styles refer to eggs cooked in hot water in their shells. Despite the word "boiled," eggs cooked in their shells should never be boiled. Boiling toughens eggs and causes discoloration. Instead, the eggs should be simmered for 12–15 minutes. Sometimes the shell is difficult to remove from very fresh eggs. Eggs that are a few days old are better for cooking in the shell. To remove cooked shells, crack shells gently on a hard surface, and remove them under cool tap water.

Red, White, and Blue Slaw

Creamy coleslaw is a requirement for barbecue. For those who think traditional coleslaw can't be improved, I say, "try this version!" Sweet, tangy, creamy, crunchy—and if you add the garnish of blue cheese, pungent too! This slaw satisfies taste on several levels. Toasting nuts really brings out their flavor, so don't skip that step. (See page 133 for toasting tips.)

This slaw is best if tossed, covered, and refrigerated a few hours before serving. However, it can be made one day ahead; wait to add blue cheese the day it is served.

Serves 10–12

1	16-ounce package classic coleslaw (shredded green cabbage and carrots)
1	10-ounce package shredded red cabbage
1 ½	cups seedless red grapes, cut in half
1/2	cup chopped walnuts, toasted
1/2	cup crumbled blue cheese (optional)

Dressing

1	cup mayonnaise
1/2	cup sour cream
2	tablespoons fresh lime juice
1/2	teaspoon freshly grated lime peel
2	tablespoons sugar
1	teaspoon celery seed
1	teaspoon salt
1/2	teaspoon freshly ground black pepper

1. In a large bowl, whisk together dressing ingredients. Add coleslaw mix, cabbage, grapes, and walnuts. Toss well.

2. Cover and refrigerate 2–6 hours.

Citrus Zest

Small but mighty! Just a bit of citrus zest—the peel of a lemon, lime, orange, or grapefruit just on the surface of the fruit—adds a real punch of flavor to a dish. Use a very fine grater, like a *Microplane*, to grate the top layer of peel. The white pith below the skin is bitter, so grate with caution!

All-American Cherry Pie

Talk about freedom of choice! This liberal cherry pie recipe lets you decide: streusel topping or star-struck pastry crust? Fruit pie is best the day it is made, but don't worry—this won't last long.

If you have baking stones to use in the oven, use them here or with other fruit pies. The heat of the stones helps bake the bottom crust. Heat stones on the lowest rack of the oven. No baking stones? Place the pie on a cookie sheet in the oven. Either way, be sure to place a piece of foil larger than the pie directly underneath to catch any drips.

Serves 8-10

3   16-ounce bags frozen, dark, pitted cherries, unsweetened

1   cup red fruit juice—cranberry, cran-raspberry, or cherry

1/3   cup cornstarch

1   cup sugar

1/2   teaspoon salt

1/2   teaspoon almond extract

1   refrigerated piecrust, such as **Pillsbury**

    Streusel Topping (see page 177)

1. Preheat oven to 375 degrees.

2. Thaw frozen cherries slightly in a strainer over a bowl, about 15 minutes. Place drained cherries in a large mixing bowl.

3. In a large saucepan over medium-low heat, cook fruit juice, sugar, cornstarch, and salt, stirring constantly until quite thick, about 2–4 minutes. Stir cornstarch mixture into cherries. Add almond extract, and mix well.

4. Fit pastry into 9-inch deep-dish pie plate. Fold under edges and crimp. Add cherry filling. Top with Streusel Topping.

5. Place pie on a cookie sheet lined with aluminum foil (to catch any drips) on the lowest rack of oven. Bake for 1 hour to 1 hour and 10 minutes, or until filling is bubbling around the edge and the crust and streusel are browned.

6. Transfer pie to wire cooling rack. Let cool at least an hour—until pie is almost at room temperature—before cutting into wedges to serve.

Streusel Topping

The pecans in the streusel topping are not toasted first; they will toast in the oven as part of the topping.

---

1   cup all-purpose flour

1/2   cup packed light brown sugar

1   teaspoon ground cinnamon

6   tablespoons (3/4 stick) butter, cut into small pieces

3/4   cup pecans, chopped

1. In a small mixing bowl, combine flour, brown sugar, and cinnamon. With fingertips, work in butter until medium-size crumbs form.

2. Add chopped pecans to the flour mixture, and toss with a spoon until the pecans are evenly distributed.

Festive, Two-Crust Pie

Use two refrigerated piecrusts. Follow the recipe, placing the filling in the crust. Place the second crust on a work surface. Using a small star cutter, cut a pattern of stars from the second crust. Carefully lift and place the crust on the pie. Fold under the edges, and crimp. Brush crust edges with beaten egg white, and place cutout pastry stars around the edges. Brush top of crust and stars with beaten egg white. Sprinkle with about 2 tablespoons sugar. Bake as directed on page 176.

Quick Tricks with Refrigerated Piecrusts

❋ Look for ready-made piecrust dough in the refrigerated dairy case of the supermarket, usually near the butter and margarine. Let piecrust dough stand at room temperature for 15–20 minutes before unrolling. To prevent tearing as well as shrinkage when baking, avoid pulling and stretching the dough when fitting in the pie plate, but do press firmly against the bottom and sides to eliminate any air pockets that might push the crust out of shape. If the dough should crack or tear before baking, dampen fingertips with cool water, and press the torn edges together.

❋ Bake refrigerated and frozen piecrusts in a glass pie plate—it absorbs the radiant heat of an oven, unlike shiny metal or aluminum pie pans that reflect heat and can prevent the bottom of the crust from browning.

❋ Cut the crust with decorative cookie cutters, and brush with melted butter. Sprinkle with cinnamon sugar, and follow the package directions for a baked piecrust. You'll have quick and delicious cookies!

❋ Using a large round cookie cutter or biscuit cutter, cut several circles, and bake according to package directions for a baked piecrust. Cool and layer the crusts between sweetened strawberries, and finish off with a dollop of whipped cream. Instant strawberry shortcake!

Red Raspberry and Blueberry Freezer Jam

This jam makes a wonderful, patriotic party favor to send home with your guests.

Yield: 5 ½-pint jars

5	8-ounce freezer jars, clean and dry
1	package **Ball Fruit Jell** freezer-jam pectin
1½	cups sugar
2	cups red raspberries, crushed
2	cups blueberries, crushed

1. In a medium bowl, combine pectin and sugar, stirring to blend evenly.

2. Add raspberries and blueberries. Stir mixture for 3 minutes. Serve immediately, if desired.

3. For longer storage, fill **Ball** freezer jars, leaving 1/2-inch headspace. Apply lids.

4. Let stand until thickened.

5. Refrigerate for up to 3 weeks, or freeze.

Bettering the Box

An Idea for Boxed Cake Mix with American Flair

Yield: 2 cups

- White cake mix
- Red and blue food color
- Red, white, and blue sprinkles

1. Prepare cake mix according to package directions.

2. Divide the prepared batter into three bowls.

3. In one bowl, add red food color and stir to combine.

4. In the second bowl, add blue food color and stir to combine.

5. Line a muffin tin with festive baking papers.

6. Fill 1/3 of each baking paper with the white batter, 1/3 with the blue batter, and 1/3 with the red batter. The entire baking paper should only be 2/3 full to prevent the baked product from spilling out of the paper as it bakes.

7. Take a butter knife and swirl the batters together.

8. Bake according to package directions.

9. Ice with prepared white frosting, and top with red, white, and blue sprinkles.

"Berry" Patriotic Candle Centerpiece

Few things mark special occasions like candlelight. So on nights when the sky is full of fireworks, why not bring a little of that glow to the table too?

The only materials you need for this pretty project are a heat-proof plate or dish, a pillar candle, and an assortment of colorful berries or small fruits. Select a star-shaped dish or any decorative, shaped dish to coordinate with a patriotic theme. Don't be concerned if the dish has a colorful pattern on it. The berries conveniently hide the design that's on the plate.

To begin, place the candle in the center of your plate. Then simply arrange the fruit around the base of the candle. Consider piling raspberries, blueberries, strawberries, and cherries around a white candle to fit a red, white, and blue color scheme. The number of berries you'll need will vary with the size of your dish and how full you make your arrangement.

Parties with Panache

❀ Red, white, and blue—the obvious choices for a July festival. Red tablecloths topped with blue glass vases that have been stuffed with white daisies or white hydrangeas set the "all-American" tone for fun.

❀ Disassemble the vases of flowers and make them into small, take-home bouquets. Tie with a blue-and-white checked ribbon.

❀ Place large, clear-glass bowls of blueberries and strawberries around your serving area.

❀ Fill small wooden produce baskets (found at craft stores) with strawberries and blueberries and give them as gifts.

❀ Serve iced-down, baby *Coca-Colas* in glass bottles for a nostalgic touch.

❀ Serve your foods in white wicker baskets lined with red and blue bandanas or old *Coca-Cola* crates.

❀ Play hits from some of the best-known American musicals. Throw in a few patriotic tunes for fun.

August

Get the Chill On

Menu

Smooth Salmon Mousse

Shrimp Gazpacho

Cool 'n' Creamy Cucumber Soup

Sweet 'n' Savory Six-Layer Dip

Creamy Fruit Freeze

Grasshopper Pie

I feel a recipe is only a theme, which an intelligent cook can play each time with a variation.

—Madame Benoit

Fresh. Frozen. Fancy. The hottest month of the year calls for foods with a chill. Simple yet satisfying, make-ahead meals make the mark when the heat is on. A unique blend of spices, yet with a cool-to-the-palette feel, makes this group of recipes a perfect blend of flavors to satisfy any hungry, heat-surviving soul.

Choose a recipe or two, and then fill in the rest of your menu with easy options like baked bagel and pita chips. Add a fruit or cheese tray.

Wine Time

Sweltering weather calls for lighter-alcohol wines. Look for German white wines—Mosel (J J Prum) or Rhine wines (Piesporter Michelsberg Kabinett). Consider sparkling white wine, such as Spanish cava (Segura Viudas Reserva Heredad), Italian Mionetto Prosecco, or an Italian rosé (Muga).

Smooth Salmon Mousse

Simple ingredients come together to create interesting combinations and complex flavors. A quick turn in the food processor creates this sophisticated first course or appetizer to serve with crackers.

Yield: 1 cup

2	3-ounce vacuum-packed packages pink salmon
2	teaspoons fresh lemon juice
1	teaspoon freshly grated lemon peel
2	teaspoons balsamic vinegar
2	tablespoons butter, softened
1/4	teaspoon salt
1/2	teaspoon freshly ground black pepper
	fresh dill or fresh parsley sprigs, to use as garnish

1. Place all ingredients, except the garnish, in the bowl of the food processor. Process until smooth. Scrape down the sides of processor bowl.

2. Remove to serving bowl. Serve immediately—garnished with fresh herbs and a generous grind of the pepper grinder—or cover and refrigerate up to 4 days. Remove from refrigerator an hour before serving.

3. Serve with breadsticks, crackers, or crisp vegetables.

Variation:

Substitute a 5-ounce package of seasoned tuna, such as **StarKist Tuna Creations**. *Try substituting tuna in flavors like zesty lemon pepper or hickory smoked in place of the two packages of salmon.*

Shrimp Gazpacho

This cold, hearty, no-cook soup is a classic from the region of Andalusia in southern Spain and has been adopted far and wide. It calls for considerable chopping, but that's it for kitchen labor. This version is "beefed up" with cold shrimp. Chill to allow flavors to mingle, then serve and enjoy!

Look for "IQF"—individually quick-frozen—shrimp in the freezer case to guarantee seafood with very fresh flavor.

Serves 6 (1 ½ cups per serving)

4	large ripe tomatoes, peeled, cored, seeded, and diced (see page 190)
1	small green pepper, seeded and diced
1	cucumber, peeled, seeded and diced (see page 137)
1	small sweet onion, minced (Vidalia or Maui)
2	cloves garlic, crushed
3	cups thick tomato juice
1	cup chicken broth
1	8-ounce bottle clam juice
2	tablespoons fresh minced chives
1/4	cup red wine vinegar
1/4	teaspoon hot pepper sauce
1/2	teaspoon salt
1/4	teaspoon freshly ground black pepper
1	pound fully cooked, peeled shrimp, chopped, or 1 pound "salad" shrimp (smaller shrimp, no need for chopping)

---

1. In a large bowl, stir together all ingredients except shrimp. Cover and refrigerate several hours or overnight to allow flavors to blend.

2. Ladle soup into six soup bowls. Top each bowl with a few shrimp.

Cool 'n' Creamy Cucumber Soup

When the weather is sweltering, you'll be refreshed by this cooling and soothing soup. Sautéed cucumber maintains its fresh, green flavor, and the lime, jalapeno, and cilantro jazz it up considerably. A bit of tangy sour cream makes the soup extra satisfying. Garnish with additional cilantro, if desired, and add diced cherry tomatoes for a sweet touch of red.

Cold temperatures dull flavors, so be sure to taste the soup before serving and adjust the salt and pepper.

Yield: 7 cups

1/2	medium onion, thinly sliced
3	medium cucumbers, about 12 ounces each, peeled, seeded and thinly sliced (see page 137 for peeling and seeding cucumber)
1	tablespoon butter
1	14 ½-ounce can chicken broth
1/2	teaspoon salt
1/4	teaspoon white pepper
1	jalapeno chili, seeded and minced
1/2	cup fresh cilantro, coarsely chopped (substitute Italian (flat leaf) parsley, if desired)
1/2	cup sour cream

1. In a large saucepan, sauté onion and cucumber in butter until cucumber is translucent, about 5 minutes.

2. Add broth. Bring to a boil, and lower heat. Cover and simmer about 5 minutes, or until onion and cucumber are quite tender. Remove from heat and cool slightly.

3. Purée mixture in batches in the bowl of a food processor or blender. Add salt and pepper. Stir in the jalapeno and cilantro, and whisk in the sour cream.

4. Cover and refrigerate until cold, at least 2 hours. Taste for seasoning, adding more salt or pepper if desired.

Sweet 'n' Savory Six-Layer Dip

Cool and colorful with a surprise punch of chili and mango, this sweet 'n' savory, dig-in dip will satisfy even heat-withered appetites. For a less hearty, meatless version, substitute 1 ½ cups shredded lettuce for the shredded chicken, and toss the lettuce with lime-cilantro dressing before adding to the layered dip.

Yield: 4 cups

1	8-ounce package cream cheese
1	15-ounce can black beans, rinsed and drained
3	green onions, sliced
	Mango Chili Salsa (see page 160)
1 ½ –2	cups poached and shredded chicken in lime-cilantro dressing (see page 199; use 2 chicken breast halves)
2	tablespoons roasted, salted sunflower seeds

1. Spread cream cheese on a dinner-size serving plate. Top with black beans, onions, mango chili salsa, chicken salad, and sunflower seeds, arranging each in smaller concentric circles.

2. Serve with crackers, tortilla chips, or vegetable dippers (jicama, carrot, celery, and zucchini).

Tomato Time

To peel and seed tomatoes: With a sharp knife, make a small "X" in the bottom of each ripe tomato. Holding tomatoes with a pair of tongs, dip in boiling water just long enough to loosen the skin (about 10 seconds). Remove from hot water, and plunge into ice water or run under cool tap water. The skin should slip off. Cut tomatoes in half, and gently squeeze to remove seeds. Drain cut-side down on paper towels.

Creamy Fruit Freeze

Fruit and ice cream make a happy pair, especially when blended into a cool, creamy treat. Use a total of 5–6 cups of fruit with 1 pint of ice cream in this easy frozen dessert. Substitute raspberries for strawberries, use cantaloupe instead of peaches, use all blueberries—it's hard to go wrong!

Prepare before dinner and enjoy that night.

Yield: 5 cups

1   pint vanilla ice cream, softened
      (leave at room temperature 15 minutes)

1   tablespoon freshly grated orange peel

1   8-ounce can crushed pineapple, undrained

2   medium ripe peaches, peeled and pitted

2   cups fresh strawberries, hulled, or
      1 10-ounce package frozen, sweetened
      strawberries, thawed

1. Place all ingredients in the bowl of a food processor. Process until smooth.

2. Pour into 2-quart freezer container. Cover and place in freezer for 2–4 hours. Scoop into dessert bowls, and serve immediately. Store any leftovers covered in freezer.

To serve remaining fruit freeze:

Leave overnight or up to 2 weeks in the freezer. The creamy fruit freeze will be frozen solid. To serve, let stand at room temperature 20–30 minutes until you can break it into chunks with a heavy spoon. Whirl in food processor until smooth. Serve at once.

Cook's note:

To hull a strawberry, cut it in half and remove the white core.

Grasshopper Pie

Don't be fooled by the title of this recipe—this chocolatey, minty pie is sure to keep your guests hopping for more!

Serves 8–10

1 ¼	cups (30–40) crushed chocolate wafers, such as **Nabisco**
1/3	cup butter, melted
20	large marshmallows
1/3	cup crème de menthe
2	cups whipping cream

1. Mix wafers and butter, and press into a 9- or 10-inch pie pan, covering the bottom and sides.

2. Chill in the freezer for about 20 minutes.

3. In a medium saucepan, melt marshmallows and crème de menthe over low heat. Cool. Whip the whipping cream (see recipe on page 87), and add to marshmallow mixture. Place the filling in the piecrust, and freeze until ready to serve. Garnish with crushed cookie crumbs or mini chocolate chips.

Cook's note:

Use 2 drops of green food coloring to give the pie a good green color. Store remaining pie in freezer.

Homemade Crumb Crusts

Type of Crust	Amount of Crumbs	Sugar	Butter, Melted	Bake
Graham cracker	1 ½ cups (24 squares)	1/4 cup	1/3 cup	yes
Chocolate wafer	1 ¼ cups (20 wafers)	1/4 cup	1/4 cup	no
Vanilla wafer	1 ½ cups (30 wafers)	none	1/4 cup	no
Cream-filled chocolate	1 ½ cups (15 cookies)	none	1/4 cup	no
Gingersnap	1 ½ cups (24 cookies)	none	1/4 cup	yes
Macaroon	1 ½ cups	none	1/4 cup	yes
Pretzel*	1 ¼ cups	1/4 cup	1/2 cup	no

*Use in a greased pie plate

In a mixing bowl, combine the crumbs and sugar (if using). Add the melted butter, and blend well. Press the mixture onto the bottom and up the sides of an ungreased, 9-inch pie plate. Refrigerate for 30 minutes before filling, or bake at 375 degrees for 8–10 minutes or until crust is lightly browned. Cool on a wire rack before filling.

Parties with Panache

* Dampen and chill fluffy, white washcloths in the freezer. If the heat is sweltering, use a cloth to refresh yourself.

* Make snow cones—adult-style! Purchase some shaved ice, or make your own in the blender. Splash the ice with your favorite wine cooler, and enjoy a relaxing, chilled drink.

* Load up a clean wheelbarrow with lots of ice and fill with flavored bottles of water.

* Frozen grapes work wonders for a cool-down. Place washed grapes on a cookie sheet, and freeze them. Serve frozen grapes with appetizers or as an accompaniment to your dessert.

* Pour fresh pink lemonade into colorful plastic cups. Place in the freezer until slushy. Serve with crazy straws.

* Buy festive colored, handheld fans to pass out to your guests to help beat the heat.

* Serve creamy fruit freeze in purchased waffle-cookie bowls for a delicious and appealing presentation.

* Serve Shrimp Gazpacho and Cool 'n' Creamy Cucumber Soup in speckled enamelware mugs. Enamelware is inexpensive and can be found at major hardware stores.

Tailgates and Paper Plates

Menu

Tailgaters'
Chicken Tortilla Wraps

South of the Border
Tenderloin Sandwiches

Santa Fe Corn and Bean Salad

Tropical Fruit Salad Cha-Cha

Pico De Gallo
with Baked Flour Tortilla Chips

Cinnamon Nachos and Fruit Salsa

Virgin Sangria

*A good cook is like a sorceress
who dispenses happiness.*

—Elsa Schiaperelli

Weekend after weekend, fired-up football fans flock to the stadium parking lots in loaded-down sport utility vehicles—with their families in tow. The camaraderie of old friends and classmates is one goal of the age-old tradition of tailgating. Achieving alfresco ambiance on the asphalt is the other.

Plan a fun and festive theme to create the mood and set the pace for the whole tailgating experience. As with any outdoor entertaining, use the unexpected to add spice to the meal.

Wine Time

Whether a tailgate or a picnic, the occasion calls for a wine that's pleasant and doesn't command a lot of attention. Try a light-bodied Chenin Blanc from South Africa (Niel Joubert) or Beaujolais-Villages (Louis Jadot) for this unique menu. A couple of other reds perfect for this menu are Saturday Red (in the one-liter jug) and Belvedere Jest Red.

Tailgaters' Chicken Tortilla Wraps

Tortilla wraps are a convenient, one-handed sandwich to serve at a tailgate or other outdoor affair. Slice wraps in half or in quarters, and arrange them on a serving platter with South of the Border Tenderloin Sandwiches. For information on how to create a wrap, see page 272.

Yield: 12

6	skinless, boneless chicken breast halves, poached
	Lime Cilantro Dressing
1 ½	8–ounce packages cream cheese, softened
3/4	cup hot pepper jelly
12	8-inch flour tortillas (try one of the flavored varieties widely available)

1. In a small bowl, stir together cream cheese and jelly.

2. Spread 2 tablespoons cream cheese mixture onto each tortilla.

3. Top with 1/2 cup chicken mixture (to make the chicken mixture, shred chicken and toss with lime cilantro dressing).

4. Roll up and wrap tightly in plastic wrap.

5. Refrigerate until packing to take to tailgate site.

Lime Cilantro Dressing

1	cup fresh cilantro, chopped
4	tablespoons lime juice
4	tablespoons olive oil
1	clove garlic, crushed
1/2	teaspoon ground cumin
1	teaspoon salt
1/2	teaspoon crushed red pepper flakes

In a medium bowl, whisk together all ingredients.

Poaching Chicken

Poached chicken is a useful ingredient to have on hand for salads, sandwiches, or casseroles, or to slather with barbecue sauce and heat briefly on the grill.

Simmer chicken in canned broth or water to which chopped celery (2 ribs), 1 onion, and 1 bay leaf have been added. Cook chicken to an internal temp. of 170 degrees (20–30 minutes). Do not boil, or the meat will toughen. Alternatively, poach chicken in a covered casserole dish (in chicken broth with vegetables) in a 350 degree oven. In a pinch, chicken can be simmered in water or broth only, with no vegetables.

South of the Border Tenderloin Sandwiches

Separately pack and tote the makings for these irresistible pork sandwiches, then make them fresh on your tailgating site. Roast the tenderloins ahead of time, order the small sandwich buns from the supermarket bakery, pick up shredded cabbage in the produce section, and stir together the simple ingredients for this snappy sauce that tops these two-bite treasures. Watch these disappear as quickly as you make them!!

You'll find pork tenderloin sold two to a package at the self-service meat counter.

Yield: 18–24

2	whole pork tenderloins, about 1 pound each
2	tablespoons chili powder
2	teaspoons light brown sugar
18–24	small sandwich buns or dinner rolls
1 ½	cups shredded cabbage (angel hair coleslaw mix)

1. Preheat oven to 450 degrees.

2. Pat tenderloins dry with paper towels. Stir together the chili powder and the brown sugar, and rub on all surfaces of tenderloins. Place the tenderloins in shallow roasting pan. Roast for 20 minutes, or until a meat thermometer inserted into the tenderloins reads 150 degrees.

3. Transfer pork to a cutting board, and let it rest at least 15 minutes before slicing into 1/4-inch thick slices. If making ahead of time, slice the pork, wrap it, and store in the refrigerator.

4. Place a couple of slices of pork tenderloin on a bun, add some shredded cabbage, and top with a spoonful of Cool and Spicy Sauce (below).

Cool and Spicy Sauce

In a small bowl, stir together 1/2 cup each of your favorite barbecue sauce and ranch dressing (such as **Hidden Valley Ranch** or Buttermilk Ranch Dressing, on page 107), 2 tablespoons chopped cilantro, and 1/2 teaspoon hot pepper sauce with chipotle, such as **Tabasco** chipotle hot pepper sauce.

Santa Fe Corn and Bean Salad

This festive salad is a riot of colors, flavors, and textures. Conveniently, it can be made ahead—up to four days. If keeping in the refrigerator, add more cilantro just before serving to punch up flavor and freshen color.

For a smoky flavor, use *Tabasco* chipotle sauce in place of regular hot pepper sauce, or for a milder flavor, use *Tabasco* jalapeno sauce.

Yield: 8 cups

1	15-ounce can black beans, rinsed and drained
1	15-ounce can pinto beans, rinsed and drained
1	11-ounce can *Green Giant Mexicorn*
1	11-ounce can mandarin oranges, drained
1/2	cup each: red, green, and yellow bell pepper, seeded and finely diced
1/2	cup sweet onion, diced (such as Vidalia or Maui)
1/4	cup chopped fresh cilantro

Dressing

1/4	cup cider vinegar
3	tablespoons orange juice
2	tablespoons canola oil
2	teaspoons freshly grated orange peel
1/2	teaspoon ground cumin or chili powder
1/2	teaspoon hot pepper sauce, such as *Tabasco*
1/2	teaspoon salt

1. In a large bowl, place beans, corn, mandarin oranges, peppers, onion, and cilantro.

2. In a medium bowl, whisk together all dressing ingredients. Pour over bean mixture.

3. Cover and refrigerate the mixture for up to four days.

Tropical Fruit Salad Cha-Cha

An explosion of color and almost too pretty to eat, this will become a staple in your repertoire of party dishes that can go just about anywhere. Vary the fruit depending upon the season, what's available, and what looks good to you. Including pineapple, mango, kiwi, star fruit (carambola), or coconut—or all of these—merits this fruit salad its "tropical" name. The amount and proportions of fruit are up to you and how many you're serving. Count on at least 1 ½ cups of fruit for every guest.

Serves 6-8

Mango, cubed or diced

Pineapple, cored and cubed, or one 11-ounce can pineapple chunks, drained

Kiwi fruit, peeled and sliced 1/4-inch thick

Carambola (star fruit), sliced 1/4 inch thick

Green or red seedless grapes, rinsed

Blueberries, rinsed

Cantaloupe, cubed

Seedless watermelon, cubed

Flaked coconut and/or fresh mint leaves

Orange Syrup

1. In a large serving bowl, combine friut and gently toss together.

2. For every 8 cups of fruit, prepare one recipe of the Orange Syrup, and pour over fruit.

3. Cover and refrigerate for several hours or overnight. Garnish with flaked coconut and/or fresh mint, if desired.

Orange Syrup

1	cup orange juice
1/4	cup sugar
1	teaspoon freshly grated orange peel
1	teaspoon vanilla extract

1. Stir together orange juice and sugar until sugar dissolves.

2. Stir in grated orange peel and vanilla.

Preparing Mango

The mango contains a big, spherical pit. To best use the fruit, peel mango with a sharp paring knife. Stand the peeled mango on one end, and slice it along one side, cutting as close to the center as you can. Turn mango and slice off other side. This will yield two usable pieces of mango fruit. To remove as much remaining fruit as possible, cut around the pit with a paring knife, and remove irregular pieces of mango. Dice all fruit to use as desired. One medium-to-large mango will yield about 3/4 cup diced fruit.

Pico De Gallo with Baked Flour Tortilla Chips

Literally "rooster's beak" in Spanish, pico de gallo is a relish made of finely chopped ingredients. Culinary legend reports that the name comes from the action of eating with the fingers—the back-and-forth motion from bowl to mouth is like the pecking beak of a rooster. You'll probably want to use a spoon or tortilla chip for scooping up this all-purpose condiment.

Use plum or beefsteak tomatoes for this jazzy salsa. Just make sure the tomatoes are ripe and full of flavor. Try squeezing the tomatoes over the sink to remove as many seeds as possible before dicing. (See page 137 for peeling and seeding cucumbers.)

This is a free-form recipe. Feel free to substitute vinegar for lime juice. Add minced fresh orange, jicama, or shredded carrot, and use green onion instead of red. If you're a fan of fiery food, try a habanero chili instead of a jalapeno (substitute 1 habanero for 1 jalapeno).

Yield: 3 ½ cups

1	pound ripe tomatoes (plum, cherry, or beefsteak), seeded and finely chopped
1	cup red onion, finely chopped
6	tablespoons fresh cilantro, minced
1/4	cup fresh lime juice
2	cloves garlic, crushed
1–2	tablespoons seeded jalapeno chilies, minced
	salt and fresh black pepper to taste

1. In a medium bowl, stir together all ingredients.

2. Season with salt and pepper to taste, then let stand for at least 30 minutes to allow the flavors to blend.

Cooking with Chilies

Hot chilies—jalapeno, serrano, and habanero—add personality to dishes, but they're worthy of healthy respect when handling. Oils from the chilies linger on skin for hours; wear disposable gloves when seeding and chopping. The heat (capsaicin) is found in the seeds, ribs, and throughout the flesh. To de-seed and de-rib, cut the chili in half lengthwise, strip out the inner ribs and seeds with the tip of a sharp paring knife, and discard ribs and seeds.

Baked Flour Tortilla Chips

Homemade tortilla chips—what a treat! These delicious chips are worth the extra effort. Store baked chips in a tightly covered container for up to 3 weeks.

Yield: 32

2	8 ½-ounce packages 6-inch flour tortillas
1/2	cup olive oil
	salt

1. Preheat oven to 375 degrees.

2. Place the tortillas in a single layer on baking sheets coated with cooking spray. Brush lightly with olive oil on both sides.

3. With a knife or kitchen shears, cut each tortilla into 4 wedges. Sprinkle each wedge with salt.

4. Bake for 8–10 minutes, or until crisp and light brown. Cool slightly. Chips will continue to crisp as they cool. Serve warm or at room temperature.

Great Way to Spray

When preparing your tortillas for baking, open your dishwasher. Yes, the dishwasher! Hold the baking sheet inside the dishwasher and apply the cooking spray. This saves your cabinets and floors from being coated, too.

Cinnamon Nachos with Fruit Salsa

This recipe is a snap to pull together. The jewel tones of the fruit and the hint of cinnamon is a perfect combination for satisfying your tailgating sweet tooth. If you don't have time to prepare a dessert, order cookies in your team colors. The local bakery will be glad to help!

Yield: 32

8	10-inch flour tortillas
1/2	cup butter, melted
1/2	cup sugar
1	teaspoon cinnamon

1. Preheat oven to 400 degrees.

2. Combine sugar and cinnamon.

3. Place the tortillas in a single layer on parchment-lined baking sheets. Brush lightly with melted butter, or spritz them with butter-flavored cooking spray.

4. With a knife or kitchen shears, cut each tortilla into four wedges. Sprinkle each wedge with cinnamon sugar.

5. Bake until crisp and golden brown. Chips will continue to crisp as they cool.

Fruit Salsa

Yield: 2 cups

1/2	cup strawberries
1/2	cup kiwi, chopped
1/2	cup mandarin oranges, chopped
1/2	cup blueberries
1/4	cup apple jelly
1/8	cup fresh mint, chopped

1. Chop fruits finely.

2. In a medium bowl, combine all fruits.

3. Melt apple jelly, and fold it into fruits, along with the chopped mint.

4. Serve with cinnamon nachos.

Virgin Sangria

This is a refreshing drink on its own, splashed over ice. You might also want to offer a bit of "boost" to guests by adding an ounce or two of dry red wine, brandy, dark rum, bourbon, or vodka. Plan ahead of time to freeze pineapple, grapes, or melon—use the frozen fruit instead of ice to keep the drinks chilled.

Yield: 12 6-ounce servings

1   32-ounce bottle cranberry juice cocktail, chilled

1   12-ounce can frozen pineapple-orange juice concentrate, thawed

1   28-ounce bottle club soda, chilled

     about 8 cups frozen fruit "cubes"

1. In a large drink container, mix all ingredients well.

2. Keep chilled, and serve over frozen fruit cubes. If desired, add 1 ½ ounces brandy, rum, bourbon, vodka, or dry red wine to each serving.

Cook's note:

To make fruit cubes, simply cube the melon or pineapple, and freeze it in a single layer on a baking sheet (grapes may be placed on the sheet whole). When frozen solid, store the fruit cubes in a self-sealing plastic bag in freezer.

Parties with Panache

* Just because you're outside tailgating doesn't mean you're obligated to use paper. Cloth napkins—whether coolly elegant, white linens or bright bandanas—add a special touch. Plus, they're a more pleasant way to deal with messy fare.

* Place napkins under a football so they don't blow away.

* Use plastic tumblers and paper plates in your team colors.

* Chill the wine in a big ice-filled football helmet lined with plastic.

* Use a Mexican poncho to dress up the back of your tailgate.

* Place chips in sombreros.

* Have your guests wear team colors.

* Assign a party referee. Have a person in a referee shirt throw the yellow flag for the following offenses: holding—holding on to the chips too long; party foul—double dipping anything.

Octoberfeast

Menu

Mustard-Pepper Crusted Pork Loin Roast
with Apple Cider Chutney

Roasted Butternut Squash
and Apple Soup

Glorious Green Beans
and Onions with Bacon

Autumn Pear Salad
with Toasted Walnuts and Goat Cheese

Herbed Baguette Breadsticks

Peppered Parmesan Breadsticks

Pumpkin Butterscotch Cake

Garlic is the ketchup of intellectuals.

—Anonymous

Crisp winds, falling leaves, and pumpkins lining the front porch—October. This is the month to usher in the holiday season. Heartier blends of familiar spices offer satisfying suppers as the days shorten for the winter season. Rich, warm soups, roasted nuts, and tart apples hasten all to the harvest table. This month's recipes offer endless possibilities for creating the perfect dining experience.

Wine Time

The hints of sweet in this menu—the squash, the pork, and the salad—call for a fruity white (Becker Chardonnay), a Pinot Blanc Alsace (Trimbach), or a spicy, peppery Zinfandel (Perry Creek Zin Man).

Roasted Butternut Squash and Apple Soup

This velvety soup is brimming with the colors and flavors of autumn. Serve in small portions as a first course, or turn it into a whole meal with the addition of grilled ham-and-Swiss cheese sandwiches on rye bread. You can roast the squash a day or two before (mash and refrigerate). In fact, this soup is a great candidate for make-ahead status.

Cover and refrigerate leftover cooked, mashed squash (after measuring the 3 cups you'll need for this soup) for up to four days. Serve squash as a simple dish for roast meat or poultry. Reheat gently in a saucepan with a little chicken broth. Season with salt and pepper, and serve with pat of butter.

Yield: 9 cups

1	butternut squash, about 3–4 pounds
1	tablespoon canola oil
2	cups onion, chopped
1	tablespoon fresh ginger root, grated
2	crisp green apples (such as Granny Smith), peeled, cored, and cut into chunks (about 2 cups)
3	14 ½-ounce cans chicken broth
1	teaspoon salt
1/2	teaspoon freshly ground black pepper
1	teaspoon fresh thyme leaves (or use 1/2 teaspoon dried thyme)
1	cup light cream (half-and-half)

Cook's note:

If you are not a fan of ginger, leave it out of the soup. It will be delicious either way.

1. Preheat oven to 400 degrees.

2. Cut squash lengthwise. Remove seeds and place cut side down on a nonstick baking pan. Pour 1/4 cup water into the pan, and roast for 45 minutes, or until squash is tender when stuck with the tip of a knife or a fork.

3. Remove from oven. Scoop cooked squash into medium bowl (discarding peel), and mash with a fork.

4. In a large saucepan, heat oil, and sauté onion, ginger, and apples, stirring for about 5 minutes, or until onion begins to brown. Measure 3 cups of mashed squash into the saucepan. Stir in broth, salt, pepper, and thyme, and bring to a boil. Reduce heat and simmer, covered, for about 15 minutes to allow flavors to blend.

5. Purée in batches in a food processor or blender. Return to saucepan and reheat. Stir in cream and serve, or make ahead without adding cream. Refrigerate covered for up to two days. Stir in cream, reheat gently, and serve.

Autumn Pear Salad with Toasted Walnuts and Goat Cheese

Flavors, textures, and colors combine for a salad that celebrates the fall season. Ripe pears, red grapes, goat cheese, and toasted walnuts are arranged atop a bed of baby salad greens finished with mustard vinaigrette. This stylish salad makes any dinner special.

Serves 6

6	cups mesclun greens (baby salad greens), cleaned
3	large ripe pears (such as Bartlett or Comice), cored and sliced into wedges
1 ½	cups seedless red grapes, rinsed and halved
3/4	cup crumbled goat cheese
1/4	cup chopped walnuts, toasted (see page 133 for instructions for toasting nuts)

Vinaigrette

3	tablespoons red wine vinegar
3	tablespoons extra virgin olive oil
1	tablespoon Dijon mustard
1/2	teaspoon sugar
1/4	teaspoon salt
1/4	teaspoon freshly ground black pepper

1. Arrange 1 cup greens on each of six salad plates. Arrange pear wedges and grapes equally among salads. Top with goat cheese and toasted walnuts.

2. In a small bowl, whisk together vinaigrette ingredients (or see page 97 for Raspberry Vinaigrette) and drizzle over salads. Serve immediately.

Variation:

Use blue cheese in place of the goat cheese.

Mustard-Pepper Crusted Pork Loin Roast with Apple Cider Chutney

Although delicious year-round, pork roast especially says "autumn," and when accompanied by an apple side dish, such as this easy spicy chutney, it's perfect for a dinner party. Boneless pork loin is a cinch—simply slice and serve! And today's much leaner pork cooks more quickly than your grandmother's pot roast. Here it's coated with a mustard-pepper paste and browned in a very hot oven to begin, then the oven temperature is lowered to finish the pork to perfection.

Serves 8

1	3 ½–4 pound boneless pork loin roast
3	tablespoons butter, room temperature
2	tablespoons Dijon-style mustard
1	tablespoon dry mustard
1	tablespoon freshly ground black pepper
1	tablespoon light brown sugar
2	teaspoons dried thyme

1. Preheat oven to 450 degrees.

2. Pat the pork dry with paper towels. In small bowl, mix together butter, Dijon, and dry mustards, pepper, sugar, and thyme. Spread paste on the top and sides of pork.

3. Place pork in a shallow roasting pan, and roast for 20 minutes. Reduce heat to 350 degrees, and continue roasting for 30 minutes to 1 hour, or until internal temperature, measured with a meat thermometer inserted into thickest part of pork, is 160 degrees.

4. Remove pork from oven (internal temperature will continue to rise). Cover loosely with foil, and let rest for 10 minutes before slicing to serve, accompanied with Apple Cider Chutney (see page 216).

Apple Cider Chutney

This chutney recipe is not only the perfect accompaniment to the mustard-pepper pork loin roast, but you may also want to serve it over a block of cream cheese with crackers for dipping.

Yield: 3 ½ cups

1/2	cup apple cider
1/4	cup cider vinegar
1/4	cup packed light brown sugar
1/2	teaspoon ground cinnamon
1/4	teaspoon allspice
1/4	teaspoon dry mustard
1/4	teaspoon crushed red pepper
3	large (about 1 ¼ pounds total) tart apples (such as Granny Smith), peeled, cored, and chopped in 1/2-inch pieces (about 3 cups)
1	cup dried cherries (sweet or tart) or raisins

1. In a medium saucepan, bring to a boil cider, vinegar, sugar, cinnamon, allspice, and mustard. Cook over high heat, uncovered, for 3 minutes; stir constantly.

2. Add apples and cherries. Reduce heat to medium-low, and simmer until apples are tender but not falling apart, about 10–15 minutes.

3. Remove from heat. Stir in red pepper. Serve warm or chilled. To store (if made ahead or if you have remaining chutney), cover and refrigerate.

Glorious Green Beans and Onions with Bacon

This dish is a great, dressed-up-for-company version of just about everybody's favorite green vegetable. Onion and bacon make perfect flavor companions with many vegetables, particularly green beans.

Do-ahead tip: Prepare steps 1–3 up to 2 hours ahead; set aside. About 10 minutes before serving, reheat the onion mixture in a skillet and proceed.

Serves 8 (3/4 cup each)

1½	pounds fresh green beans, ends trimmed
6	slices bacon
1	16-ounce package frozen pearl onions, thawed and drained
1	tablespoon sugar
3/4	teaspoon dried thyme
2	tablespoons cider vinegar
1	teaspoon salt
3/4	teaspoon freshly ground black pepper

1. In a large saucepan, bring water to a boil. Add beans and cook until just tender, about 6–7 minutes. Drain.

2. In a large skillet, cook bacon until crisp. Remove bacon from pan, reserving 2 tablespoons bacon drippings in the pan. Crumble bacon and set aside.

3. Add onions to bacon drippings. Cook, stirring, for 3 minutes over medium heat. Add sugar, and stir 3–4 minutes more, or until onions are golden brown.

4. Stir beans into skillet, and cook, stirring, for 1–2 minutes or until beans are heated through. Add vinegar, salt, and pepper. Toss to coat. Just before serving, stir in crumbled bacon.

Herbed Baguette Breadsticks

Culinary triage to the rescue of day-old bread! This recipe is custom made for that stale loaf of sourdough or French bread. Slice bread thickly, then cut crosswise into thick fingers or sticks. Brush with herbed olive oil, and these come to life in the oven. You'll make these often as a perfect accompaniment to a soup meal or to pair with main dish salads. And you don't have to start with stale bread!

Serves 8

1	12-inch baguette, sliced 1/2-inch thick
1/3	cup olive oil, or amount needed
2	teaspoons minced fresh herbs: thyme, oregano, or chives

1. Preheat oven to 375 degrees.

2. Cut bread slices into 1-inch-wide sticks.

3. In a small bowl, stir together oil and herbs. Brush cut surfaces of bread with the olive oil mixture. Place sticks on a baking sheet.

4. Bake for 15–18 minutes, or until golden brown. Serve warm.

Peppered Parmesan Breadsticks

Homemade breadsticks hot from the oven? No sweat—with the help of dough from the freezer section. Nothing is more tempting than the smell of baking bread, so treat yourself to these easily made breads often.

Egg whites beaten lightly with a little water are a baker's friend, as this mixture helps to brown baked goods, helps additions adhere (like the cheese and black pepper in this recipe), and gives a glossy look to golden-brown treats from the oven.

Yield: 12

1	1-pound loaf frozen white bread or pizza dough, thawed according to package directions
	nonstick cooking spray
1–2	tablespoons cornmeal
1/4	cup grated Parmesan cheese
2	tablespoons freshly ground black pepper

1. Preheat oven to 425 degrees.

2. Spray baking sheet with nonstick cooking spray. Sprinkle lightly with cornmeal. Set aside.

3. With rolling pin, roll dough into a 7x10-inch rectangle. Cut into twelve 7-inch strips. Gently twist each strip, and place 1 inch apart on the prepared baking sheet. Brush each breadstick with egg white. Carefully sprinkle with Parmesan and pepper.

4. Bake 12–15 minutes, or until golden brown. Transfer to wire rack. Serve warm.

Pumpkin Butterscotch Cake

This moist cake is reminiscent of a steamed pudding—perfect for a dinner party during autumn's chill. Allow the cake to cool in the pan for at least 30 minutes before removing it.

While preparing cake batter, roast chopped pecans by placing them on a baking sheet in the 350-degree oven for about 3–5 minutes.

Because it's so moist, this cake needs no frosting, so just serve with a dusting of powdered sugar. To dust cake (or other desserts) with powdered sugar, place a spoonful of powdered sugar in a small strainer (like a tea strainer), hold the strainer over cake, and tap the edge of strainer with spoon.

Serves 8–12

2	cups all-purpose flour
1 ¾	cups sugar
1	tablespoon baking powder
1 ½	teaspoons ground cinnamon
1	teaspoon salt
1/2	teaspoon ground nutmeg
1/2	teaspoon ground cloves
1	15-ounce can pumpkin (not pumpkin pie mix)
3	large eggs
1	teaspoon vanilla extract
1	11-ounce package butterscotch-flavored chips
1	cup chopped pecans, toasted
	powdered sugar

1. Preheat oven to 350 degrees.

2. Spray a 12-cup, nonstick **Bundt** pan with cooking spray, and dust well with flour. Sprinkle all interior surfaces of the pan with flour; shake pan well, moving in a circular motion to coat all surfaces with a light dusting of flour. Knock out and discard excess flour.

3. In a medium bowl, combine flour, sugar, baking powder, cinnamon, salt, nutmeg, and cloves.

4. In a large bowl, whisk together pumpkin, eggs, and vanilla. Stir in flour mixture to blend thoroughly, and stir in butterscotch chips and pecan pieces.

5. Spoon batter into prepared pan, and bake for 60–70 minutes, or until wooden pick inserted in the cake comes out clean.

6. Remove from oven, and cool in the pan on a wire rack for 30 minutes. Remove cake from pan, and cool completely. Serve slices sprinkled with powdered sugar.

Baking Bonus Tips

Effortless Sifting

If using a sifter makes your wrist ache and uses too much of your precious time, try whisking the ingredients to be sifted instead. Since the purpose of sifting is simply to infuse the dry ingredients with enough extra air to guarantee a fluffy result, whisking for 1 minute can do the trick without the work. Another option is to sift using a handheld, wire-mesh strainer. Pour dry ingredients through the strainer and, holding it over a mixing bowl, gently tap its side.

Fast Flouring

Fill a saltshaker with flour, and store it in the freezer. (The flour won't freeze, but you'll prevent bacterial growth during long-term storage.) The next time a recipe calls for flouring the pan after it's been greased, grab your shaker. A few flicks of the wrist will make your pan batter-ready while keeping your work surfaces spotless.

Eggshell Extraction

When a shell fragment finds its way into your bowl of batter, forget using your fingers to chase the slippery shell around. Instead, just dip a clean eggshell in. The stray fragment will latch on like a magnet.

Parties with Panache

* Baskets, baskets, and more baskets—full of pinecones, mini pumpkins, fall squash, gourds, and eucalyptus.

* Set scarecrows, pumpkins, hay bales, and other fall-themed items around your home—both inside and out.

* Personality pumpkins. Give your plain pumpkins personality with paint pens, or add a bit of style by gluing dried flowers and herbs on top with a hot glue gun. Use whatever you have on hand to make your pumpkins shine.

* For a fancy look, spray paint a pumpkin using matte gold spray paint. Sponge on silver paint. Group several of these together on your dining room table with votive candles nestled in between, giving your dining room table a lovely look.

* Mum's the word. Pots full of mums make the signature fall foliage flourish. All sorts of colors, blooms, and styles add to your fall theme. The front porch, backyard, or favorite area in your home will say "Fall is here!" with a colorful bloom.

* Fall-ish front doors. Indian corn tied together with a raffia bow makes an autumn statement like no other. Fall colors glisten in the husks and welcome guests with a unique warmth.

November

Harvest Holiday

Menu

Spice-Brined Roast Turkey Breast

Home-style Corn Bread Dressing
with Fruit and Pecans

Green Peas, Prosciutto,
and Red Peppers

Mashed Sweet Potatoes with
Maple Syrup and Pecan Streusel

To invite a person into your home is to take charge of his happiness for as long as he is under your roof.

—Brillat-Savarin

Thanksgiving is my favorite holiday—cooler temperatures, crisp leaves, and porches lined with pumpkins. Coming from a family where food plays a big role in any get-together, I can close my eyes and smell the celery for the corn bread dressing simmering in real butter and the yeast wafting through the kitchen as the rolls rise for the second time.

Thankfulness, gratitude, and favorite foods are the cornerstones of life, especially at Thanksgiving. As you enter the holiday season as a newly married couple, you may want to begin to think about what traditions you want to implement in your family. Try keeping a basket in your breakfast room. Place a pen and paper scraps in the basket. Every time you have a "blessing" in your day, write it down, and keep it in the basket. On Thanksgiving morning, sit down a moment and review the "good things" you and your husband have experienced. What are you thankful for, and how does your family share gratitude during this wonderful time of year?

Wine Time

The traditional American Thanksgiving menu with its hearty, homey flavors marries perfectly with either a red or white wine, so have both on hand to offer at the table. A Pinot Noir (Saintsbury Garnet) is a sturdy red choice. A full-bodied California Chardonnay (Estancia) or a dry Gewurztraminer (Hugel) from the Alsace region of France is a tasty holiday menu choice for white wine lovers. You might also consider a sparkling Shiraz from Australia (Fox Creek Vixen) for at-the-table toasting.

Home-Style Corn Bread Dressing
with Fruit and Pecans

This dressing is one you'll make often. Colorful, flavorful, and full of textures, it pairs well with roasted poultry, a ham dinner, or pork roast. It's worth making your own corn bread a few days ahead and letting it stale slightly. From scratch or from a mix, corn bread is tasty on its own—hot from the oven—or as a soup or stew accompaniment.

If making the dressing ahead of time, cover and refrigerate overnight. Increase initial baking time to 30 minutes.

Serves 8–10

1	cup dried apples
2	tablespoons canola oil
1 ½	cups chopped onion
1	cup chopped celery
8	cups crumbled corn bread (see page 230)
1	cup chopped pecans
1/2	cup dried apricots, diced (see page 161)
1/2	cup canned chicken broth
1	tablespoon dried sage leaves
1	teaspoon dried thyme
1/2	teaspoon dried, crushed rosemary
1	teaspoon freshly ground black pepper
2/3	cup canned chicken broth

1. Preheat oven to 375 degrees.

2. In a small bowl, place apples. Cover with warm water, and let soak 10 minutes. Meanwhile, in a large skillet, heat oil, and sauté onion and celery until soft, about 7–8 minutes.

3. Drain apples and chop. Place in a large bowl with onion and celery, crumbled corn bread, pecans, apricots, 1/2 cup broth, herbs, and pepper. Mix well, and place dressing in a 13x9x2-inch dish.

3. Bake for 15 minutes. Spoon remaining 1/2 cup broth over dressing, and bake for 20 minutes, or until dressing is heated through.

Spice-Brined Roast Turkey Breast

A whole turkey breast, from 6 ½–7 pounds, provides enough white meat for about 6–8 people. You might want to roast two whole turkey breasts or opt for tackling the whole bird (see page 229).

Why brine? Turkey (and turkey breast in particular) can easily dry out during roasting. Brining the bird (a brine is simply a marinade made with water, sugar, and salt) introduces more moisture to the bird before roasting, resulting in a moister turkey at the table. Instead of a whole turkey breast, you might want to roast one or two turkey breast halves (sometimes called a "split half") each weighing about 2 pounds, which will cook more quickly than a whole breast. Prepare as below, reducing roasting time to 45 minutes to an hour.

Serves 6–8

Brine

1/3	cup salt
1/4	cup packed light brown sugar
4	cloves
4	whole allspice
1	tablespoon whole peppercorns
2	bay leaves
1	bone-in turkey breast
1	tablespoon butter, softened
1	teaspoon freshly ground black pepper

1. Place salt and brown sugar in a heavy-duty plastic bag or a resealable, 2-gallon bag large enough to hold the turkey breast. Stir in a couple cups of water, stirring until salt and sugar are dissolved. Add cloves, allspice, peppercorns, bay leaves, and turkey breast. Add enough water to just cover turkey. Seal bag. Turn bag gently a few times to thoroughly coat the turkey with brine. Refrigerate 2–6 hours, turning occasionally.

2. Preheat oven to 375 degrees.

3. Remove turkey from brine. Discard brine. Rinse turkey well, and pat dry. Place turkey skin-side up in a shallow roasting pan. Rub all surfaces with butter, and sprinkle with pepper.

4. Roast (bake) for 1 hour 10 minutes to 1 hour 30 minutes, or until internal temperature (measured with a meat thermometer inserted into thickest part of breast) reads 170 degrees. The internal temperature of a turkey breast will continue to rise from the residual heat in the breast, even after you take it out of the oven. This is known as carryover cooking time. After the first 30 minutes of roasting, start basting (use a pastry brush) turkey breast with pan juices every 10–15 minutes; basting results in a nicely golden-brown surface.

5. Remove from oven. Loosely cover turkey breast with foil, and let stand 10–15 minutes so the juices within the breast meat can redistribute, creating a juicy, moist turkey breast.

6. To carve the turkey breast, first remove breast halves from the bone. With a sharp knife, cut vertically on either side of the breastbone, as close to the bone as possible, angling the knife around the wishbone. Remove each breast half to the cutting board, and slice across grain to the thickness you desire.

Standing time for roasts:

Why "standing time"? When you remove a meat or poultry roast from the oven, allowing it to stand for 5–20 minutes (depending on the size of the roast) allows the juices to redistribute and "slow down" (they've been racing around inside the meat during the roasting process). Cutting into a roast immediately will result in the loss of those delicious, moist, flavor-carrying juices. Standing time can be very convenient for the cook, too, as it allows you to finish the last-minute details of dinner.

Turkey, Dressing, and Cranberry Wraps

It's a "wrap in a snap" with leftover turkey.

Serves 4–6

4–6	flour tortillas (7–10 inch), room temperature
2	cups cooked turkey, diced or shredded
2	cups prepared corn bread stuffing
1	16-ounce can whole berry cranberry sauce

1. Heat turkey and stuffing if desired. Divide turkey and stuffing, and place on tortillas.

2. Top with approximately 2 tablespoons cranberry sauce.

3. Fold or roll up to enclose filling.

Tackling the Big Bird

There are many resources to help you successfully roast, carve, and serve the whole bird. If this exciting culinary challenge is calling you, check out the National Turkey Federation's Web site, www.eatturkey.com, or call the Butterball Turkey Talk Line (800-288-8372), Reynolds Turkey Tips Line (800-745-4000), or the USDA Meat and Poultry Hotline (800-535-4555).

Corn Bread

Yield: 8 cups

1	cup cornmeal
1	cup all-purpose flour
4	teaspoons baking powder
1/2	teaspoon salt
1/4	cup sugar
2	large eggs, beaten lightly
1/4	cup canola oil
1	cup milk

1. Preheat oven to 400 degrees.

2. Lightly spray an 8-inch baking pan with nonstick cooking spray. In a medium bowl, stir together cornmeal, flour, baking powder, salt, and sugar.

3. Beat eggs, oil, and milk together. Add all at once to dry ingredients, and stir until blended.

4. Turn batter into the prepared pan. Bake for 20–25 minutes, or until lightly browned.

5. Remove from oven. Turn bread out onto cooling rack. Cut into squares to serve warm with butter and cane syrup, if desired. If using corn bread for dressing, let cool to room temperature, crumble coarsely (roughly 1/2-inch pieces), and let stand overnight—covered loosely—to dry.

Green Peas, Prosciutto, and Red Peppers

Festive, colorful, and full of flavor, this vegetable dish steals the show with sweet peas and bell peppers joining flavor forces with cured prosciutto (dried Italian ham), onion, and celery. The sweetness of the vegetables is countered by a touch of vinegar just before serving.

Serves 8–10

2	tablespoons extra virgin olive oil
1/4	cup onion, minced, or 2–3 shallots, peeled and sliced
1	stalk celery, minced
1	large red bell pepper, seeded and sliced into 1/8-inch thick, 2-inch long pieces
2	1-pound packages frozen peas
2–3	ounces (about 5–6 paper-thin slices) prosciutto, diced
2	tablespoons fresh chives or marjoram, minced
1/4	teaspoon salt
1/2	teaspoon freshly ground black pepper
2	teaspoons white wine vinegar

1. In a large skillet, heat oil over medium heat. Sauté onion, celery, and pepper until onion softens, about 4 minutes.

2. Stir in peas and prosciutto. Cook and stir until peas are heated through. Stir in fresh herbs. Season with salt, pepper, and vinegar. Serve hot.

Mashed Sweet Potatoes with Maple Syrup and Pecan Streusel

If you're a sweet potato lover, this is your dish! Maple-kissed sweet potato purée is topped with a crunchy streusel topping for a dish that's a perfect addition to roast turkey, pork, or ham.

Make-ahead tip: Prepare up to one day ahead. Store covered in the refrigerator. If baking from refrigerator temperature, add about 10 minutes to baking time.

Serves 6–8

1/2	cup packed light brown sugar
1/4	cup chopped pecans
2	tablespoons unsalted butter, cut into small pieces
4	large sweet potatoes, scrubbed and pierced in several places with a sharp knife
2	large eggs, beaten
2	tablespoons pure maple syrup
1	tablespoon vanilla extract
1 ½	teaspoons fresh lemon juice
1	teaspoon salt

1. Preheat oven to 400 degrees.

2. Place potatoes directly on the oven rack, and bake for an hour to an hour and 10 minutes, or until the potatoes can be pierced easily with a paring knife.

3. Remove potatoes from oven. Split in half, and scoop flesh into large bowl. Mash by hand with potato masher. Alternatively, place in food processor, and process by pulsing gently. Remove potato purée to large bowl. Stir eggs, syrup, vanilla, lemon juice, and salt into potatoes.

4. Mix sugar, pecans, and butter in a small bowl. Set aside.

5. Place potato mixture in a 9x13-inch (2–3 quart) baking dish. Sprinkle evenly with pecan topping.

6. Bake until set and the topping bubbles, about 1 hour. Let stand 15 minutes before serving.

Parties with Panache

❊ Fall leaves, ceramic turkeys, persimmons, pomegranates, and mini pumpkins combined on a mantel say "Thanksgiving" loud and clear.

❊ Pilgrim statues, Indian corn, and colorful squash make a great, front door entry combo to set the stage for what awaits your guests inside.

❊ Classical music wafting through your home says, "Stay awhile, relax, and fill your plate with seasonal fare."

❊ Natural materials such as fall leaves, pinecones, twigs, sage-green pumpkins, and gourds can be combined with your own candlesticks, small potted plants, or flowers to create beautiful seasonal displays.

❊ Using an odd number of candles in seasonal colors and adding fall greenery, you can make a pretty and impressive Thanksgiving table.

Holidays by Design

Menu

Spicy Cocktail Meatballs
with a Trio of Dips

·

Tomato and Herbed Cheese Tart

Crostini and Pita Chips
with Three Dips

Goodie Gifts in Jars

Address yourself to entertain them sprightly,
and let's be red with mirth.

—Shakespeare

Heart, hearth, and home all play a part in holiday celebrations. The spirit of the season comes into full bloom when you unpack the holiday boxes and begin to deck the halls. The bright decorations, shiny ornaments, and fragrant greenery somehow always manage to turn an ordinary home into an extraordinary winter wonderland, especially nice when preparing the foods for a holiday get-together. This chapter is made complete with mix-and-match dips for easy entertaining and simple food gift-giving ideas, garnished with packaging options.

Wine Time

For an open house, plan to have a couple of different red and white wines to accommodate the tastes of your guests. Offer both a sturdy red like a Pinot Noir (Fess Parker) and a softer Cabernet from California (Knights Valley) or Merlot from Chile (Montes Alpha). Serve a round Chardonnay from New Zealand (Stoneleigh) or California (Rombauer) and a crisp French Sauvignon Blanc (Pascal Jolivet). And don't forget a sparkling wine (Roederer or S. Anderson) for toasting the season.

Tomato and Herbed Cheese Tart

This quiche-like tart can be served as an appetizer, first course, or even as an entrée for a luncheon. Spread an herbed cheese in the crust, top with colorful sun-dried tomatoes and fresh basil, add smoky bacon and a savory custard, and bake. This tasty tart delivers big flavors for little kitchen labor.

Serves 6–8

1   refrigerated piecrust, such as **Pillsbury**

1   egg white, whisked with 1 tablespoon water

1   6 ½-ounce package garlic and herb-seasoned spreadable cheese, such as **Alouette**

1/2   cup thinly sliced sun-dried tomatoes, not oil-packed

1/4   cup chopped fresh basil

5   slices bacon, cooked crisp and crumbled

3   large eggs

1/2   cup milk

1/2   teaspoon salt

1/2   teaspoon freshly ground black pepper

1.   Heat oven to 425 degrees.

2.   Fit the pie crust into a 9-inch pie pan. Fold under the excess dough and crimp. Prick the bottom with a fork. Bake 5 minutes. Remove from oven.

3.   Reduce oven temperature to 375 degrees.

4.   Brush the bottom of the crust with egg white. Spoon cheese by dollops into the bottom of piecrust, roughly spreading (it is not necessary to have cheese perfectly spread). Sprinkle tomatoes, basil, and bacon over cheese.

5.   In a medium bowl, whisk together eggs, milk, salt, and pepper. Pour over mixture in crust.

6.   Bake until bubbling and crust is nicely browned, about 20–25 minutes. Cool slightly, slice into wedges, and serve warm or at room temperature. If made ahead, store covered in the refrigerator for up to one day.

Tart Tips

Look for vacuum-packed (not oil-packed) dried tomatoes on the supermarket shelf or in the produce section.

Brushing the bottom of the unbaked crust with egg white creates a seal, keeping the bottom crust crisp.

Spicy Cocktail Meatballs with a Trio of Dips

These perfectly seasoned meatballs are almost addictive. They are the perfect make-ahead hors d'oeuvres. These easy meatballs brown quickly in the oven and can be frozen or refrigerated until ready to serve. They are irresistible served with a variety of dips.

Arrange the meatballs on a platter with sliced red or green bell pepper, or pile them in a pretty serving bowl with a few clusters of red or green seedless grapes.

Yield: 80 ¾-inch meatballs

1 ½	pounds lean ground beef (90 percent lean)
1/2	pound lean ground pork
1	cup milk
1/2	cup fresh whole-wheat bread crumbs (from slightly more than 1 slice bread—see page 241)
1 ½	teaspoons salt
1/2	teaspoon ginger
1/2	teaspoon allspice
1/2	teaspoon ground cayenne (red pepper)
1/4	teaspoon freshly ground black pepper
5	green onions with some green top, minced
1	tablespoon unsalted butter

1. Preheat oven to 500 degrees.

2. In a large bowl, mix (by hand) beef, pork, milk, bread crumbs, salt, ginger, allspice, cayenne, and black pepper. Let stand 5 minutes.

3. Sauté onion in butter in small skillet until just soft, about 1 minute. Add to meat mixture. Mix thoroughly.

4. Shape mixture into very small balls, about 1 rounded teaspoon each. Place in a shallow, rimmed baking pan, such as a 15x10x1 jelly roll pan.

5. Bake until lightly browned, 10–15 minutes. Drain, cover, and refrigerate up to two days. For longer storage, place cooled meatballs in a self-sealing plastic bag. Freeze up to one month.

6. Serve warm or at room temperature with one or more of the dips on page 241.

Sweet, Savory, and Spicy Dips for Meatballs

Cranberry Barbecue Dip. In a medium bowl, stir together 1/2 cup each whole berry cranberry sauce and smoky, tomato-based barbecue sauce.

Bacon-Blue Dip. In a medium bowl, beat together an 8-ounce package cream cheese (softened), 2 tablespoons half-and-half (light cream), 1/4 cup crumbled blue cheese, 2 tablespoons chopped chives, and 1/3 cup crumbled, crispy bacon.

Creamy Curry Dip. In a medium bowl, stir together 1/2 cup mayonnaise, 1/2 cup sour cream, 1 tablespoon lime juice, and 2 ½ teaspoons curry powder (taste to determine "more or less," depending upon the heat of the curry powder you use). Season with salt if desired, and add a pinch of cayenne (ground red pepper).

Fresh Bread Crumbs

To make fresh bread crumbs, trim crust from firm sandwich bread, tear bread into pieces, and process in food processor until coarse crumbs form. One slice of bread makes about 1/3 cup crumbs.

White Bean Hummus

Hummus is a thick dip usually made with chickpeas, lemon juice, garlic, and olive oil served Middle Eastern style with pita chips and breadsticks. Throwing a different spin on a traditional dip, this recipe substitutes canned white beans for chickpeas and adds fresh herbs. Although it seems like a simple dish, it has an interesting taste. You'll agree as you watch this dip disappear.

Yield: 3 cups

2	15 ½-ounce cans great northern or cannelloni beans, rinsed and drained
3	cloves garlic, minced
1/4	cup lime juice
2	tablespoons extra virgin olive oil
2	tablespoons fresh basil, chopped
1	tablespoon fresh chives, chopped
1	teaspoon salt
3/4	teaspoon freshly ground black pepper

1. In a food processor or blender, purée beans with garlic, lime juice, and oil. Remove to medium bowl, and stir in herbs. Season with salt and pepper.

2. Serve at room temperature with crackers, breadsticks, pita chips, crostini, and/or veggies.

Crostini:

Slice 2 (12-inch) long baguettes to about 1/2-inch thick. Cut garlic clove in half and rub one side of each bread slice with the cut side. Brush the garlic side of each bread slice lightly with olive oil, and sprinkle with coarse salt. Oven broil until browned, about 1–2 minutes. Turn and broil the other side until brown. This can be made one day ahead. Store in airtight container.

Pita chips:

Heat oven to 450 degrees. Slice 4 8-inch plain pita breads into 8 wedges. Divide each piece in half at the "seam." Place pita wedges in a large bowl and toss with 1/3 cup olive oil, coarse salt, and freshly ground black pepper. Spread in a single layer on a rimmed baking pan. Bake for 5–8 minutes, stirring a couple times for even browning, until lightly browned and crisp. Make up to one day ahead. Store in airtight container.

Green Fire Dip

This intriguing dip tastes rich and spicy. Besides making a great holiday match with Roasted Red Pepper and Garlic Dip, this dip also makes a delicious accompaniment for grilled shrimp or roasted chicken wings. The amount of jalapeno to add to this dip depends upon your taste for "heat."

Yield: 3 cups

3	cups coarsely chopped fresh cilantro (about 2 bunches)
2–4	jalapeno chilies, stemmed, seeded, and coarsely chopped (see page 204)
1	large bunch green onions, including some green tops, chopped
2	teaspoons salt
2	cups sour cream

1. Process the cilantro, chilies, green onions, and salt in a food processor until fairly smooth. Remove to a medium bowl.

2. Whisk sour cream into cilantro mixture until smooth. Taste, and adjust salt.

3. Serve immediately with tortilla chips, crackers, breadsticks, pita chips, crostini, or veggies—or refrigerate up to five days.

Roasted Red Pepper and Garlic Dip

The beautiful red hue of this dip is festive, and when you pair it with green veggies for dipping, you're in the holiday spirit immediately!

Roasting garlic or bell peppers is an invaluable kitchen skill you'll use time and again. Roasting garlic mellows it considerably and brings out its sweetness, and you'll find many uses for it.

Yield: 2 ½ cups

5	cloves garlic, unpeeled
1	teaspoon olive oil
3	red bell peppers, seeded, roasted (see page 133), and peeled
4	ounces cream cheese, softened
1	tablespoon lemon juice
3/4	teaspoon salt
1/2	teaspoon freshly ground black pepper

1. Preheat oven to 400 degrees.

2. Place garlic cloves on small piece of heavy foil. Drizzle with oil. Seal foil packet, and bake until garlic is soft, about 30 minutes.

3. Remove garlic from oven, unwrap, and squeeze garlic from cloves into food processor or blender. Add remaining ingredients, and pulse to blend thoroughly.

4. Adjust salt and pepper to taste. Cover, and refrigerate. Serve with crackers, breadsticks, pita chips, crostini, or veggies.

Goodie Gifts in Jars

Say "happy holidays" with a homemade treat—no cooking required! When you give a gift with a gathered-together mix, the recipients will think of you again when they enjoy a freshly made muffin or a mug of hot cocoa. What do you put in the jars? The next few pages have recipes for creating delicious, festive goodie jars.

* Use jars with interesting shapes for these mixes. Check out the supply at a hobby or craft store, gourmet kitchen store, or rummage sale (if you keep your eye out at garage sales year round, you'll have a nice supply by holiday time).

* Trim lids with burlap, squares of colorful kitchen towels, or holiday-designed fabric.

* Use butcher's twine or kitchen string in place of ribbon. Create your own gift tags by cutting up last year's holiday cards. Punch a hole in them, and thread twine or ribbon through the hole.

* Write the recipe down on a festive 4x6-inch index card decorated with holiday stamps or stickers. Your recipient will now be able to make the goodie gift again!

Polka-Dot Brownies in a Jar

What a great gift to have stashed away in your pantry when a quick, homemade dessert is needed.

Yield: 1 quart

1	cup plus 2 tablespoons all-purpose flour
1/2	teaspoon salt
1/2	teaspoon baking powder
1/3	cup unsweetened cocoa powder
2/3	cup sugar
2/3	cup packed light brown sugar
1/2	cup semisweet chocolate chips
1/2	cup white chocolate chips

Additional ingredients for later use

3	large eggs
2/3	cup vegetable oil
1	teaspoon vanilla extract

1. In a small bowl, combine the flour, salt, and baking powder. In a 1-quart glass container, layer the flour mixture, cocoa, sugar, brown sugar, and white and chocolate chips (combined in one layer), packing well between each layer.

2. Cover; store in a cool dry place for up to six months.

3. Attach the following recipe.

To prepare brownies:

In a large mixing bowl, beat the eggs, oil, and vanilla. Add brownie mix and mix well. Pour into a greased, 8-inch square baking pan. Bake at 350° for 26-28 minutes or until center is set (do not overbake). Cool on a wire rack.

Fajita Seasoning Mix

This recipe is sure to please your Fajita-loving friends and family.

Yield: 1/4 cup

1	tablespoon cornstarch
2	teaspoons chili powder
1	teaspoon paprika
1	teaspoon sugar
3/4	teaspoon chicken bouillon granules
1/2	teaspoon onion powder
1/4	teaspoon garlic powder
1/4	teaspoon cayenne pepper
1/4	teaspoon cumin

1. Combine ingredients in a small, airtight container. Apply the lid securely.

2. Attach the Chicken Fajitas recipe (see page 248).

Chicken Fajitas

Serves 4

4	boneless, skinless chicken breasts, sliced into thin strips
2	tablespoons canola oil
1/3	cup water
1	green bell pepper, sliced, seeds and core removed
1	onion sliced
6	8-inch tortillas (white or corn)

1. Sauté chicken in hot oil in a 10-inch skillet for 5 minutes.

2. Add all of the fajita seasoning mix and all remaining ingredients except for tortillas. Sauté until juices run clear when chicken is pierced with a fork, about 5 additional minutes.

3. Place tortillas on a microwave-safe plate. Cover with plastic wrap, and microwave on high for 1 minue.

4. Spoon chicken mixture down center of tortilla. Roll up and enjoy!

Cranberry-Apple Chutney

When going to a holiday party, this makes a lovely hostess gift. Place in a festive jar that has been decorated for the season.

Yield: 2 cups

2	cups fresh cranberries
1	cup Granny Smith apples, cored, peeled, and chopped
2/3	cup orange juice
1/2	cup sugar
1	teaspoon freshly grated lemon peel
1	tablespoon crystallized ginger, minced

In a medium saucepan, place all ingredients. Bring to a boil. Reduce heat to low. Cover and simmer until cranberries pop and mixture thickens slightly. Store in the refrigerator.

Haute Cocoa

Gifts can be ready and waiting with cocoa to go. This inexpensive and simply packaged idea can be made ahead and tucked away for a delicious treat for the entire family. Get creative, with your favorite spices or imported chocolate to create your own signature cocoa.

Yield: 15 cups

6	cups unsweetened baking cocoa
2	cups malted milk powder
7	cups sugar
2	tablespoons cinnamon
1	teaspoon cardamom
1	vanilla bean, split in half (scrape seeds into cocoa mixture, discarding vanilla bean)

Blend all ingredients, and let sit for 3 days. Spoon into festive gift jars. Attach the following instructions.

To make cocoa:

Mix 1/4 cup of cocoa mix into an 8–10 ounce mug of hot milk.

Sweet and Spicy Pecans

These pecans make a wonderful gift for the men in your life. They can be used as a garnish for salads or as a sweet and spicy nibble before a holiday meal.

Yield: 2 cups

1/2	cup sugar
3	tablespoons water
1	teaspoon salt
1/2	teaspoon cayenne pepper
2	cups pecan halves

1. Preheat oven to 350 degrees.

2. In a medium saucepan, combine the sugar, water, and cayenne pepper. Cook over medium heat, stirring constantly until sugar is dissolved. Boil for 2 minutes. (Do not stir.)

3. Add the pecans, and stir until coated.

4. On a large baking sheet covered with foil or parchment paper, spread out pecans, and bake for about 13 minutes or until toasted. Remove to wax paper to cool. Store in a 1-pint jar or container.

Parties with Panache

To create a holiday party atmosphere, consider these ideas.

* Select a color theme. Use it on your tabletops, gift-wrappings, tree trimmings, and fresh flowers.

* Wrap your dining room table. Make it look like a HUGE package. Purchase some strong, colored wrapping paper, duct tape, and wired ribbon. Cover the table with the festive paper. Tape the ends underneath the table to create the appearance of a package. Using the wire ribbon, form a large bow. Place the bow in the center of your table.

* Fill tall, clear-glass cylinders with a mixture of nuts (in their shells) and citrus fruit. Glass containers look especially lovely filled with sparkly glass balls. Display cylinder on a mantel or dining table for a festive holiday look.

* Fabric remnants make terrific table coverings. Fold under the edges, and using a glue gun, hem the unfinished ends to create an inexpensive table topper to match your color theme. Layering these types of covers adds texture and style to your table.

* Clear-glass, vintage saltshakers make lovely bud vases. Place a fresh sprig of holly or evergreen, or a single poinsettia stem in the shaker. Tie a thin red ribbon around the grooved part of the shaker.

Breakfast, Lunch, and Dinner for Two

Breakfast

Jazzy Artichoke Eggs

Apple Dandy Syrup for Pancakes

Your Favorite Pancakes

Strawberries and Cream French Toast

Morning Magic Muffins

Santa Fe Eggs Ranchero

Bananas Foster Oatmeal

Strawberry-Banana Smoothie

Jazzy Artichoke Eggs

This elegant brunch dish is based on a New Orleans recipe for the Eggs Sardou served at Antoine's Restaurant.

Bring out the good dishes, and put on the New Orleans-style jazz to set the mood. Serve this delicious entrée with freshly squeezed orange juice and plenty of black coffee.

If you're pressed for time, fried or poached eggs work beautifully in place of the hard-cooked eggs in this dish.

Serves 2–3

1	9-ounce package frozen creamed spinach, partially thawed
1	6 ½-ounce jar marinated artichoke hearts, drained and coarsely chopped
1/4	teaspoon hot pepper sauce, such as **Tabasco**
2–3	hard-cooked eggs, peeled and cut lengthwise into halves
1/4	cup creamy Caesar salad dressing
1	tablespoon buttermilk or milk
	salt and freshly ground black pepper
	toasted bread, cut diagonally into triangles

1. In a shallow baking dish or 8 or 9-inch glass pie plate, combine the partially thawed creamed spinach, chopped artichoke hearts, and hot pepper sauce. Spread evenly in bottom of dish or pie plate.

2. Microwave (loosely covered with plastic wrap) on high power for 4 minutes, or until mixture is bubbly hot.

3. Place the hard-cooked egg halves cut-side up on top of the hot spinach mixture, pressing slighting to secure the eggs in the bed of spinach.

4. In a small cup, combine salad dressing and buttermilk. Spoon salad dressing over spinach mixture, being sure to leave some of the egg yolk showing.

5. Microwave, covered, on high power for 45 seconds— just to warm the eggs and sauce. Add salt and pepper to taste. Serve with toast triangles.

Cook's notes:

See page 174 for directions for hard-cooked eggs.

Don't turn up your nose to buttermilk! It's a versatile ingredient—it's delicious in baked products, adds a tang to salad dressings, and helps crumbs or breading adhere to foods you want to fry. Besides being available in quart and 1-cup containers, buttermilk can be purchased in powdered form. Just mix the powder with water before use.

If you want to make this dish even heartier, add diced or cubed cooked ham to the spinach mixture. Also, for a richer flavor and texture, stir 1/2 cup grated Pepper Jack or Monterey Jack cheese into the spinach mixture, along with the artichoke hearts.

Apple Dandy Syrup for Pancakes

Although other varieties of apples may be used in this recipe, Golden Delicious apples are particularly good, as they hold their shape and color when cooked. This quick and easy sauce is also great over ice cream.

Yield: 2 ½–3 cups

1	tablespoon butter
2	medium-sized Golden Delicious apples, peeled, cored and cut into 1/4-inch-thick slices
1/2	cup packed light brown sugar
1/4	cup orange marmalade or apricot preserves
2	tablespoons orange juice
1/4	teaspoon ground cinnamon

1. In nonstick skillet over medium-high heat, melt butter.

2. Add apple slices. Cook, stirring occasionally, until apple slices are tender and golden brown, about 8 minutes.

3. Add remaining ingredients, and cook, stirring rapidly, until mixture comes to a boil and sauce thickens slightly, about 2 minutes.

4. Serve over Your Favorite Pancakes (page 257) or waffles.

Your Favorite Pancakes

These pancakes will become your favorite! They're easy to make, tender, and oh-so-flavorful! If you have time to make some extras, just double the recipe. Cool the extra pancakes on a paper towel, then place them in a small plastic freezer bag, and freeze. Pop one or two in the microwave some hurried morning. Spread with a little jam, and serve with a tall, cold glass of milk.

Yield: 8

1	cup all-purpose flour
1	tablespoon sugar
1/2	teaspoon salt
1/2	teaspoon baking soda
1	large egg, beaten
1	cup buttermilk
2	tablespoons canola oil
2	tablespoons club soda or lemon-lime soda
	vegetable oil or nonstick cooking spray (for griddle)

Cook's note:

Club soda is great to have on hand to help remove red wine stains from carpet or tablecloths. It adds fun fizz to fruit juice to make a refreshing drink, and it helps make these pancakes extra tender and light.

1. In a medium bowl, combine flour, sugar, salt, and baking soda.

2. In a small bowl, blend egg, buttermilk, and the oil. Pour the egg mixture into the flour mixture. Stir quickly—just until all ingredients are moistened. Add the club soda, and stir to combine.

3. Put a teaspoon of canola oil on a nonstick griddle, or spray the griddle with cooking spray. Place griddle over medium-high heat.

4. Dip a 1/4-cup measuring cup into the batter and pour onto the griddle. The size of the griddle will determine how many pancakes you can cook at one time. Cook until small bubbles appear and begin to break on the top surface of the pancakes, and the outside edges appear set. Flip the pancakes, and cook the second side until done. If pancakes brown too quickly, lower the heat.

5. Serve with Apple Dandy Syrup (see page 256).

Pancake Variations

Nutty Pancakes. If you feel like a nut, add a flavor crunch! Stir 1/2 cup coarsely chopped pecans or walnuts into the pancake batter.

Blueberry Pancakes. Wash and thoroughly drain 1/2 cup fresh blueberries. Just sprinkle them on the pancakes as soon as you pour the batter on the griddle. If you stir the berries into the batter, they often break up and cause the batter to turn an unappetizing color.

Banana Pancakes. Place about three slices of banana on top of each pancake as soon as the batter hits the pan, or sprinkle banana slices with brown sugar and serve on top of the pancakes before you add any syrup.

Strawberries and Cream French Toast

Rich, creamy strawberry filling adds to this tasty version of a basic French toast.

Serves 2

4	slices hearty white bread, lightly toasted in toaster
2	tablespoons strawberry cream cheese spread
1	large egg
1/3	cup milk
1/2	teaspoon vanilla or almond extract
1–2	tablespoons unsalted butter
2	cups fresh strawberries, cleaned, stems removed, and sliced
	powdered sugar

1. Spread 2 of the toasted bread slices with the cream cheese spread. Top each with another bread slice to make 2 "sandwiches."

2. In a shallow bowl, beat egg, milk, and vanilla together with a fork.

3. On a hot griddle over medium heat, melt butter. Dip sandwiches into egg mixture, turning to coat both sides.

4. Cook until browned on one side, then turn and cook on the second side, approximately 2 minutes per side. Cut diagonally into triangles.

5. Serve with sliced strawberries and powdered sugar.

French Toast Variations

If strawberry cream cheese spread is unavailable, use regular cream cheese spread. Finely chop several tablespoons of sliced strawberries, and blend with the cream cheese before spreading it on the toast.

You Might Also Try:

Sunny Flavors of Citrus. Add grated orange or lemon peel to the cream cheese.

Almond-Crunch. Add 1/4 teaspoon almond extract to the cream cheese. Just before serving, sprinkle the French toast with toasted sliced almonds.

Peaches 'n' Cream, a Classic Combination. Use sliced peaches instead of strawberries.

Morning Magic Muffins

Because of their versatility, these moist, sweet muffins will always bring a "good morning" smile. One recipe . . . multiple variations . . . make-ahead directions . . . that's called kitchen magic!

This batter can be made ahead and refrigerated for up to a week. You can bake all of the batter at once and freeze the baked muffins to pop in the microwave later, or you can divide the batter into two different portions and make two different batches of six muffins each. Fun recipe variations will give each batch a different twist.

Yield: 12

2 ¼	cups all-purpose flour
1/2	cup packed light brown sugar
1/4	cup sugar
2	teaspoons baking powder
1/2	teaspoon baking soda
1/2	teaspoon salt
1	cup buttermilk
1/3	cup canola oil
1/3	cup applesauce
1	large egg

Cook's note:
This recipe is a cinch to double.

1. In a medium bowl, stir together flour, both sugars, baking powder, baking soda, and salt.

2. Combine buttermilk, oil, applesauce, and egg in small bowl. Beat with fork or whisk until mixed.

3. Add buttermilk mixture to flour mixture. Stir just until dry ingredients are moistened. Bake immediately, or refrigerate batter in a tightly covered container for up to one week.

4. When ready to bake muffins, heat oven to 400 degrees. Spray the cups of a 6-cup or 12-cup muffin pan with nonstick cooking spray, or coat cups lightly with a paper towel moistened with canola oil. Or, you may use paper baking cups. Divide batter evenly among cups, filling them 2/3 full.

5. Bake 20–25 minutes, or until muffins are golden brown. Remove muffins from baking pans. Serve warm.

Muffin Variations

Lemon-Blueberry. To the batter, add 1/2 cup fresh blueberries, rinsed and drained, and 1/2 teaspoon grated lemon peel. Bake as directed.

Banana. Stir 1 banana, finely diced, and 1/4 teaspoon ground cinnamon into the batter. Bake as instructed.

Cranberry-Orange-Almond. Stir into the batter 1/2 cup dried, sweetened cranberries, along with the grated peel of an orange and 1 teaspoon almond extract. Sprinkle tops of unbaked muffins with slivered almonds and sugar before baking. (For best results, soak dried cranberries in hot water for a few minutes. Drain thoroughly before adding to batter.) You may also use golden raisins or dried cherries.

Cinnamon-Sugar. Combine 2 tablespoons sugar and 1/4 teaspoon ground cinnamon. Brush tops of hot, baked muffins with melted butter, and sprinkle with cinnamon-sugar mixture.

Jam. Drop 1/2 teaspoon of your favorite jam into batter for each muffin. Press into batter, and bake as directed in the recipe.

Muffin Hints

Muffins stay fresh stored at room temperature in an airtight container for three days, unless made with cream cheese or other perishable foods. If made with perishable foods, refrigerate.

Filling muffin cups. Pour batter into muffin tins using a measuring cup or ice cream scoop. This helps prevent drips around the edges of the pans.

Santa Fe Eggs Ranchero

The sunny flavors of the Southwest are a wonderful way to start the weekend. This could become your special Saturday-morning treat!

Serves 2

3/4	cup mild or medium picante sauce
2	tablespoons orange juice or chicken broth
2–4	large eggs
4	corn tortillas
1/2	cup shredded Monterey Jack or cheddar cheese
	salt and freshly ground black pepper

Cook's note:

Use either 1 or 2 eggs per serving. If you cook only 2 eggs (1 per serving), reduce picante sauce to 1/2 cup.

1. In a small skillet with a lid, bring picante sauce and orange juice to a boil over medium heat. Reduce heat to keep sauce gently simmering.

2. Break and slip eggs into simmering sauce, and cook until egg whites just begin to set. Cover with lid, and cook until egg whites are completely set and yolks begin to thicken, approximately 2 minutes.

3. Place corn tortillas in paper towel lightly dampened with water. Microwave on high power for 35 seconds to soften and warm.

4. Serve cooked eggs with sauce on top of a warmed corn tortilla. Sprinkle with shredded cheese. Add salt and pepper to taste. Fold a second tortilla into quarters, and serve on the side.

Bananas Foster Oatmeal

Craving bananas Foster, but it's too early in the day for the dessert? Try this oatmeal. It will surely hit the spot!

Serves 2

2   servings of regular or quick-cooking oatmeal, prepared according to package directions

1   medium banana, sliced

2   tablespoons chopped pecans, toasted

4   teaspoons caramel ice cream topping

    milk (optional)

1. Divide topping between 2 bowls of oatmeal and microwave on high for about 15–20 seconds, or until toppings are warm.

2. Pour milk over oatmeal, if desired.

Strawberry-Banana Smoothie

Serves 2

1/2	cup milk
1	cup vanilla-flavored yogurt
1	tablespoon honey
2	cups frozen strawberries
1	ripe banana, sliced

Place all ingredients in a blender, and process until smooth. Enjoy!

Cook's note:

Keep a few peeled bananas in the freezer for use in smoothies. Frozen bananas pump up the volume of the smoothies and keep them icy cold.

Lunch

"In a Pickle" Classic Grilled Cheese

Jack Cheese and Pepper Jelly Melts

Muffuletta Panini

Herbed Cheese Wraps
with Roasted Peppers and Sprouts

Smoked Turkey and Spinach Wraps

Green Chili and Beef Roll-Ups

Middle Eastern Pita Pizzas

Asparagus and Plum Tomato Pizza

"BLT" Chicken Salad

Tortellini Salad

Crunchy Cranberry and Tuna Salad

Sandwich Grilling Guidelines

Melted cheese oozing out of the corners of a golden brown toasted sandwich is a favorite comfort food to many. A variation on the basic sandwich is included here, along with two additional creative flavor combinations.

A nonstick griddle, griddle pan, or skillet is recommended for grilling cheese sandwiches. See the suggested equipment list that begins on page 3 of this book. If you have one of the new electric sandwich makers or a panini grill, follow the manufacturer's instructions.

The cheese selected can vary also, from a mild-tasting Swiss, Monterey Jack, cheddar, or colby, to a stronger-flavored cheese such as smoked Gouda, Gorgonzola, or blue cheese. Just be sure to match the fillings and bread with the cheese selection. Hand-grated or shredded cheese melts easily, but sometimes thin, deli-sliced cheese is more convenient. Just be creative!

These recipes call for spreading softened butter on the outside of the bread before grilling. It's a great technique because if you melt butter on the griddle before adding the sandwiches, the butter will often overheat or burn before you get the sandwiches there! This way there is no wasted butter, and you end up with a sandwich with better flavor and color.

"In a Pickle" Classic Grilled Cheese

Most grilled cheese sandwiches can be assembled ahead of time, wrapped, and then refrigerated until you are ready to grill.

Serves 2

4	slices hearty white or country-style white bread
2	teaspoons Dijon mustard
4	slices cheddar or colby cheese (about 4 ounces)
8	slices bread-and-butter or dill pickles
2	tablespoons unsalted butter, softened

Cook's note:

Most store-purchased sliced bread is 1/4–1/2 inch thick. Do not use bread any thicker than that or the cheese will not melt before the bread has over-browned.

1. Place bread on cutting board. Spread each slice with 1/2 teaspoon mustard. Set 2 slices aside.

2. Place fillings on mustard-covered side of each of the 2 bread slices in the following order: 1 slice of cheese, 4 pickle slices, and a second slice of cheese.

3. Top with remaining 2 bread slices (mustard side down) to make 2 sandwiches. Spread softened butter on the outside of all bread slices.

4. On a nonstick griddle or in a large skillet, cook sandwiches over medium heat for 2 minutes or until the underside is brown. With a spatula, turn each sandwich, and press firmly for about 30 seconds to get the cheese to adhere to the bread and filling.

5. Continue cooking 1–2 minutes more, or until sandwich is golden brown and cheese is melted. Cut diagonally into halves, and enjoy immediately!

Jack Cheese and Pepper Jelly Melts

Try this spicy-sweet version of an old favorite!

Serves 2

4	slices sourdough or hearty white bread
3	tablespoons red pepper jelly
4	slices deli-sliced Monterey Jack or Havarti cheese (about 4 ounces)
4	slices deli-sliced, smoked turkey breast
2	tablespoons unsalted butter, softened

1. Place bread on cutting board. Spread each slice with about 2 teaspoons pepper jelly. Set slices aside.

2. Place fillings on jelly-covered side of each of 2 bread slices in the following order: 1 slice cheese, 1 slice turkey, and a second slice of cheese.

3. Top with remaining 2 bread slices (jelly side down) to make 2 sandwiches. Spread softened butter on the outside of all bread slices.

4. On nonstick griddle or in a large skillet, cook sandwiches over medium heat 2 minutes or until the underside is brown. With a spatula, turn each sandwich, and press firmly for about 30 seconds to adhere the cheese to the bread and filling.

5. Continue cooking 1–2 minutes more or until sandwich is golden brown and cheese is melted. Cut diagonally into halves and serve immediately.

Muffuletta Panini

Bring a little bit of the French Quarter to your kitchen with this tasty sandwich.

Serves 2

4	slices Italian bread
1/4	cup chopped olive salad, bruschetta topping, or tapenade
4	slices deli-sliced provolone, fontina, or mozzarella cheese (about 4 ounces)
4	slices deli-sliced ham or prosciutto
6	slices deli-sliced salami
1/4	cup unsalted butter, softened

Cook's note:

These sandwiches are also terrific when cooked on an electric sandwich maker or panini grill. Follow the manufacturer's directions for best results.

1. Place bread on cutting board. Spread each slice with 1 tablespoon olive salad. Set 2 slices aside.

2. Place fillings on olive salad-covered side of each of 2 bread slices in the following order: 1 slice cheese, 1 slice ham, 3 slices salami, and a second slice of cheese.

3. Top with remaining 2 bread slices (olive salad-side down) to make 2 sandwiches. Spread softened butter on outside of all bread slices.

4. On a nonstick griddle or in a large skillet, cook sandwiches over medium heat for 2 minutes, or until the underside is brown. With a spatula, turn each sandwich, and press firmly for about 30 seconds to get the cheese to adhere to the bread and filling.

5. Continue cooking 1–2 minutes more, or until sandwich is golden brown and cheese is melted. Cut diagonally into halves and enjoy immediately!

Herbed Cheese Wraps with Roasted Peppers and Sprouts

Tortillas and wraps dry out quickly when they're removed from the package, so assemble all of the ingredients you'll need before you begin preparing this recipe.

Serves 2

2	10-inch spinach-flavored flour tortillas (wraps)
1/4	cup garlic-herb cheese spread
2	thin slices deli ham or smoked turkey breast (optional)
2	roasted red peppers, split in half lengthwise and carefully dried on paper towels
1/2	cup alfalfa sprouts or mixed baby salad greens

1. Place tortillas on a large cutting board. Spread each with half of the cheese spread.

2. If using, lay one slice of ham or turkey across the bottom half of each tortilla.

3. Top with roasted red peppers, and sprinkle with alfalfa sprouts.

4. Starting at the bottom of the tortilla, roll up tightly into a spiral. Wrap in plastic wrap, and refrigerate until serving time.

Cook's notes:

Flavored cheese spreads in small tubs can be found in the dairy section of the supermarket.

Roasted red peppers are available in jars of several sizes, usually found in the supermarket near the pickles and other condiments. Once opened, the jar can be kept in the refrigerator for several weeks, or you can roast and peel your own (see page 133).

Wrap and Roll Sandwiches

These handheld, flavor-packed "sandwiches" are meals encased in flour tortillas called wraps. If you have never filled a wrap before, take time to read the "wrapology" below to make this fun adventure even easier.

* Wraps, or "gourmet tortillas," are usually found with the tortillas in the supermarket, but also are often found on a shelf near the deli counter.

* Wrap sizes vary from brand to brand, but they are usually 10–12 inches in diameter. (Rectangular flatbreads are available in some markets and may be used like wraps.)

* Wraps can be stored at room temperature until the package is opened. After opening, it is important to close the package tightly, and refrigerate any leftovers.

* Wraps should be flexible. If they start to crack or dry out, put a slightly damp paper towel around the wrap, and microwave for 5–7 seconds.

* "Less is more" when filling a wrap. Too much filling is difficult to roll and will be even more awkward to eat!

❋ Use a flavorful spread as the first ingredient to put on the wrap. Soft or spreadable cheese, plain or flavored cream cheese, hummus, seasoned butter, and mayonnaise are the most popular choices. Cover the wrap almost to the edge with the spread. Leave a border of about a half-inch.

❋ Think "flat and flexible first" when it comes to layering ingredients. For the first layer, use thinly sliced deli meats, soft or flat greens (such as Bibb or butterhead lettuce, basil, or spinach), and deli-sliced cheese. The ingredients added next can be less flexible yet should still be thinly sliced or chopped: green onions, cucumber, seeded tomatoes, and carrots.

❋ Avoid any vegetable or fruit that has too much moisture. Soggy wraps are not desirable!

❋ Place filling ingredients on a little more than half of the wrap, starting at the edge closest to you.

❋ Roll the wrap tightly into a spiral, starting on the filled side. Roll wrap tightly in plastic wrap and refrigerate.

❋ Store filled wraps in the refrigerator until you're ready to serve them, or add them to your "brown bag" for lunch.

❋ Just before serving, trim ends of wraps, if desired. Slice diagonally into halves or thirds.

Smoked Turkey and Spinach Wraps

This is deli smoked turkey at its best.

Serves 2

2   10-inch spinach or sun-dried tomato-
        flavored flour tortillas (wraps)

1/4   cup soft cream cheese
        (plain or onion flavored)

1/2   teaspoon lemon pepper

2   thin slices deli smoked turkey breast

12–14   baby spinach leaves
        (trim off any large stems)

1/2   cup shredded Monterey Jack cheese
        or other mild cheese

1. Place tortillas on a large cutting board. Spread each with half of the cream cheese. Sprinkle with lemon pepper.

2. Lay 1 slice of turkey across the bottom half of each tortilla.

3. Top each with half of the spinach leaves, and sprinkle with cheese.

4. Starting at the bottom of the tortilla, roll up tightly into a spiral. Wrap in plastic wrap, and refrigerate until serving time.

Green Chili and Beef Roll-Ups

Spice up your beef roll-up with the addition of green chilies.

Serves 2

2	10-inch spinach or sun-dried tomato-flavored flour tortillas (wraps)
1/4	cup garlic-herb cheese spread
2	thin slices deli roast beef
3	whole roasted green chilies, split in half lengthwise and carefully dried on paper towels
1/2	cup mixed baby salad greens, drizzled with 1 teaspoon Italian dressing
1/2	cup shredded Monterey Jack cheese or other mild cheese

1. Place tortillas on large cutting board. Spread each with half of the cheese spread.

2. Lay 1 slice of roast beef across the bottom half of each tortilla.

3. Top with roasted green chilies and salad greens.

4. Starting at the bottom of the tortilla, roll up tightly into a spiral. Wrap in plastic wrap and refrigerate until serving time.

Cook's note:

Roasted green chilies are available in cans and jars of several sizes. Once open, the jar can be kept in the refrigerator for several weeks.

Variation:

Green chili, avocado, and beef roll-up: top beef with thin slices of avocado (sprinkled with lemon juice) before adding chilies and salad greens. Eat these roll-ups the same day they are prepared.

Middle Eastern Pita Pizzas

Serve this with pickled, mixed vegetables and sweet banana peppers to add a nice zing. The pickled vegetables and the peppers can be found in the condiment aisle of your supermarket.

Serves 2

2	pita breads (6 inches in diameter)
1/4	cup hummus, store-bought or homemade (see page 242)
1/2	cup roasted red pepper feta cheese
1/2	small onion, sliced thin
1	cup baby spinach, chopped
1/2	cup artichoke halves, chopped (from a 14-ounce can)
1	medium plum tomato, seeded and chopped (see page 190 for seeding a tomato)
2	tablespoons sliced kalamata or black olives

1. Preheat oven to 400 degrees.

2. Place pita breads on a parchment-lined baking sheet.

3. Spread hummus on each pita bread. Sprinkle with feta cheese.

4. Top each pita with onion, spinach, chopped artichoke, tomato, and olives.

5. Bake for 8–10 minutes.

Asparagus and Plum Tomato Pizza

This is a great way to use up any leftover pesto. This is a delicious twist on pizza. Make two and have friends over for a Friday night pizza party.

Serves 2

1/2	pound thin asparagus spears
1	12-inch prepared pizza crust
1	cup prepared pesto sauce, store-bought or homemade (see pages 134 and 135)
1 ½	cups fontina cheese, diced into small cubes or shredded
2	firm plum tomatoes, seeded and diced (see page 190 for seeding a tomato)

1. Preheat oven to 400 degrees.

2. Trim tough ends off asparagus, leaving 4–5 inch-long tender tops of spears.

3. In a small skillet, boil a small amount of water and add asparagus tops. Cover skillet, and turn down heat. Simmer for 2 minutes. Cut spears into 1-inch pieces, diagonally.

4. Spread pizza crust with thin layer of pesto sauce. Place cubed fontina cheese on the top of pizza. Add a scattering of chopped asparagus and diced tomatoes.

5. Bake on a pizza stone or directly on oven rack.

6. Bake for 10 minutes, or until cheese melts and the edges of the pizza are crisp and golden brown.

Preparing Asparagus

Gently bend each stalk, which will cause the woody end to break off at just the right point. If any tough spots remain, they can be removed with a vegetable peeler.

"BLT" Chicken Salad

You won't be able to resist this special lunch or supper dish. It has all your favorite flavors packed into one great chicken salad. Keep things simple by using roasted chicken from the deli or poached chicken breasts (see poaching directions on page 199).

Serves 2

1/3	cup mayonnaise
1	tablespoon sour cream, cream, or milk
1	teaspoon Dijon or spicy brown mustard
2	tablespoons real bacon bits, or cooked and crumbled bacon
1	tablespoon finely chopped fresh basil (optional)
1 ½	cups shredded, roasted, or poached chicken
	salt and freshly ground black pepper
2	small Roma tomatoes, seeded and chopped (see page 190 for seeding a tomato)
	shredded iceberg or romaine lettuce

1. In a medium bowl, stir together mayonnaise, sour cream, mustard, bacon bits, and basil.

2. Add shredded chicken. Stir to coat chicken with dressing. Add salt and pepper to taste.

3. Gently stir in 1 chopped tomato. Reserve second tomato (chopped) for garnish.

4. Refrigerate to blend flavors until serving time. Serve chicken salad on shredded lettuce. Garnish with reserved tomato.

Salad Variations

California Cool. Place an avocado half on top of the shredded lettuce and fill with chicken salad. Or place a mound of chicken salad on shredded lettuce and arrange avocado slices around the salad.

Almost Buffalo. For a spicy chicken salad that will remind you of the flavors of buffalo chicken wings, combine 1/4 cup mayonnaise with 1–2 tablespoons red chicken wing sauce (such as *Frank's* or *Nance's*), 1 tablespoon sour cream, 1/3 cup chopped celery, and 1 ½ cups shredded, cooked chicken. Add salt and pepper to taste. Serve with celery sticks stuffed with blue cheese. If you prefer, sprinkle blue cheese over the salad, and serve celery sticks on the side.

Chicken Waldorf Salad. Combine 1/3 cup mayonnaise, 1 tablespoon sour cream, 1 tablespoon chopped fresh parsley, and 1 tablespoon lemon juice. Add 1 small cored and chopped apple, 1/3 cup chopped celery, 1/3 cup toasted chopped walnuts or pecans, and 1 ½ cups shredded, cooked chicken.

Easy Curried Chicken Salad. Combine 1/3 cup mayonnaise, 1 tablespoon sour cream, 1 tablespoon chutney or apricot preserves, and 1 tablespoon chopped fresh parsley. Stir in 1/2 teaspoon curry powder. Add 1 ½ cups shredded, cooked chicken, 1/2 cup seedless green or red grape halves, and 1/2 cup toasted, sliced almonds.

Tortellini Salad

You don't have to be Italian to appreciate this recipe, and you don't have to have an Italian neighbor to provide you with homemade tortellini! Tortellini is now available—either refrigerated or frozen—in most supermarkets nationwide. This dish is so easy to prepare, you may want to double it to take to the next potluck or neighborhood picnic.

Serves 2–3

1	7-ounce package refrigerated cheese tortellini, cooked according to package directions, drained, and cooled
1	roasted red pepper, finely chopped
1/3	cup Italian or creamy Caesar salad dressing
1	6- or 7-ounce jar marinated artichoke hearts, drained and chopped
2–3	green onions, thinly sliced
	salt and freshly ground black pepper
1/2	cup grape or teardrop tomatoes, halved
1/4	cup Kalamata or stuffed green olives (Spanish), sliced or coarsely chopped
	fresh basil leaves or baby spinach, coarsely torn
	feta cheese crumbles (optional)

1. In a medium bowl, combine tortellini, red pepper, Italian dressing, artichoke hearts, and green onions. Toss gently. Add salt and pepper to taste. Cover and refrigerate at least 1 hour to blend flavors.

2. Just before serving, add tomatoes and olives. Toss gently. Add basil leaves. (Add additional dressing, if desired, for moister consistency.)

3. Sprinkle with feta cheese crumbles, and garnish with additional basil leaves.

Cook's note:

Roasted red peppers are available in jars of several sizes, usually near the pickles and other condiments. Once opened, the jar can be kept in the refrigerator for several weeks, or you can roast and peel your own (see page 133).

Variations:

Make this into a real garden salad with the addition of frozen green peas (thawed), shredded carrots, and/or chopped zucchini.

Substitute 1/4 cup chopped, sun-dried tomatoes packed in oil for the roasted red peppers.

Substitute 1/2 small red onion (cut into slivers) for the green onions.

Pasta Portions

Use 1/2 gallon (2 quarts) of water for every 4 ounces of dried pasta. 4 ounces of dried pasta will feed two people.

Crunchy Cranberry and Tuna Salad

Sweetened dried cranberries give a "kiss" of sweetness to this salad, and the toasted pecans add not only flavor, but also a fun crunch. This delightful tuna salad is delicious served on whole wheat or hearty white bread, but also try serving it as a main course salad on a leaf of Boston lettuce, garnished with apple slices. Offer wheat crackers on the side.

Serves 2

2	tablespoons orange juice
3	tablespoons sweetened dried cranberries
1	6 or 7-ounce can or pouch solid white tuna, drained
1/4	cup mayonnaise
1/2	teaspoon grated fresh orange or lemon peel
1/4	teaspoon lemon pepper
2–3	onions, thinly sliced
2	tablespoons toasted chopped pecans
	salt and freshly ground black pepper

1. In small bowl, pour orange juice over cranberries. Set aside to soften slightly.

2. In a medium bowl, break up tuna with fork. Add mayonnaise, citrus peel, and lemon pepper. Stir.

3. Add softened cranberries with orange juice, green onions, and pecans to tuna mixture. Add salt and pepper to taste.

4. Refrigerate until serving time to blend flavors.

Cook's note:

The tuna mixture will appear very moist at first, but the tuna and the cranberries will absorb the juice.

Variations:

For an extra-crunchy salad, add 1/3 cup chopped celery.

Substitute 1/3 cup chopped white or yellow onion for the green onion. Add 1 tablespoon finely chopped fresh parsley.

Garden Herb Tuna Salad: *Combine 1 can tuna (drained) with 1/3-cup mayonnaise, 1/4 teaspoon lemon pepper, 1/2 teaspoon grated lemon peel, and 1 tablespoon lemon juice. Stir in 2 tablespoons fresh, chopped parsley or a combination of parsley, basil, and mint. Serve with tomato wedges.*

Athenian Tuna Salad: *Combine 1 can tuna (drained) with 1/3 cup mayonnaise, 1/3 cup finely chopped green or black olives, 1 tablespoon lemon juice, and 1 tablespoon capers.*

Tuna and Egg Salad: *Combine 1 can tuna (drained) with 1/3 cup mayonnaise, 1 teaspoon Dijon mustard, 1 chopped hard-cooked egg, 1/3 cup finely chopped celery, and 1 tablespoon sweet pickle relish, if desired.*

Dinner

Sassy Chicken with Rice

Pan-Grilled Chicken Satay
with Peanut Sauce

Tilapia Mediterranean

Citrus Grove Orange Roughy

Fish Dijon

Fiesta Chicken and Lime Soup

Three-Cheese and
Spinach Lasagna Roll-Ups

Chicken Roasted
with Tomatoes, Potatoes, and Olives

Crab Cakes

Sassy Chicken with Rice

Flavored with the kick of picante sauce and the richness of curry powder, Sassy Chicken will strut its way to your dinner table again and again. The heat level can be adjusted by varying the type of picante sauce or chutney used. Quick and easy to make, this tasty dish is also great reheated.

Serves 2

2	tablespoons unsalted butter
1/3	cup onion, chopped
1/3	cup celery, sliced
2	tablespoons all-purpose flour
1 ½	cups chicken broth
1/4	cup picante sauce (medium or hot preferred)
1/2	teaspoon curry powder
1	cup coarsely chopped or shredded cooked chicken
1 ½	cups cooked rice

Cook's notes:

A roasted 2 ½ pound chicken equals 3–4 cups chicken meat.

For quick rice, use the quick-cooking, in-the-bag type.

1. In a medium skillet over medium heat, melt butter. Add onion and celery. Cook, stirring, until onion is translucent.

2. Add flour, and quickly stir to coat onions and celery. Add chicken broth. Stir until mixture starts to thicken.

3. Stir in picante sauce and curry powder. Stir about 2 more minutes. Add chicken. Heat through.

4. Serve over rice with any of the suggested accompaniments.

Variations:

Use leftover deli-roasted, grilled, or even fried chicken in this recipe. If using fried chicken, remove the crisp skin before adding the chicken.

This recipe is a great way to use leftover turkey.

Accompaniments:

Sliced green onions, chopped peanuts, sweet or hot chutney, and/or crisp bacon pieces.

Pan-Grilled Chicken Satay with Peanut Sauce

Traditionally, the chicken for chicken satay is placed on skewers before grilling or broiling, but this method of using a nonstick grill pan is easier.

Serves 2

1/3	cup creamy peanut butter
2	tablespoons chicken broth or water
2	tablespoons low sodium soy sauce
2	tablespoons lime or lemon juice
1	tablespoon light brown sugar
1/4	teaspoon crushed red pepper flakes or hot pepper sauce
1	small clove garlic, minced
1	tablespoon canola oil (for marinade only)
1	whole boneless skinless chicken breast (about 3/4 pound), cut into halves
6–8	7-inch wooden skewers
	sliced green onions, chopped cilantro, and chopped peanuts for garnish

1. In a small bowl, combine peanut butter, chicken broth, soy sauce, lime juice, brown sugar, red pepper flakes, and garlic. Stir rapidly to blend ingredients. (If mixture is too thick, add more chicken broth.)

2. Remove 2 tablespoons peanut sauce, and place in small bowl. Add 1 tablespoon canola oil, and stir to combine. This will be the marinade. (Reserve remaining sauce to serve with chicken.)

3. Pound the chicken breast halves until they are approximately 1/4 inch thick. Cut the pounded chicken breast lengthwise into 2-inch strips. (Depending on the size of the chicken breast, you should get 6–8 strips.)

4. Place the chicken strips in a shallow bowl. Pour the marinade over the chicken strips.

5. Brush grids of grill pan lightly with oil. Place grill pan over medium-high heat until hot. Add chicken strips, and grill 2–3 minutes per side, or until juices run clear.

6. Thread the grilled chicken strips onto the wooden skewers (just weave the skewer in and out of the chicken once), and place on serving plates. Allow 3 skewers of chicken per serving. Serve with reserved peanut sauce. Garnish with green onions, cilantro, and peanuts.

Cook's notes:

To make pounded chicken breasts with easy cleanup, split a gallon-sized, self-sealing, plastic food-storage bag along the seams. Place the chicken on one side of the bag and cover with the other side before pounding.

Variations:

If you have any peanut sauce left over, toss it with some cold noodles, sliced cucumber, and slivered carrot, and you have a great lunch for the next day!

Get Hooked on Fish

Tilapia Mediterranean

You might call these easy-to-prepare recipes the "catch of the day." There are three different choices, depending on the ingredients you have on hand and the flavor mood you are in.

Serves 2

1	14 ½-ounce can petite-cut diced tomatoes with garlic and olive oil, or diced tomatoes with basil, garlic, and oregano
1/4	cup fresh parsley, chopped
1/4	teaspoon dried oregano leaves
1/4	teaspoon crushed red pepper flakes
2	4 to 6-ounce tilapia, orange roughy, or flounder fillets
1	tablespoon lemon juice or white wine
2–3	ounces crumbled feta cheese (about 1/3 cup)
2	cups hot cooked angel hair pasta or orzo
	chopped fresh parsley for garnish

1. Preheat oven to 400 degrees.

2. Pour tomatoes into a small, shallow baking dish. Stir in parsley, oregano, and crushed red pepper flakes.

3. Place fish fillets on top of tomatoes. Drizzle fillets with lemon juice.

4. Spoon some of the tomato mixture over the fish fillets. Sprinkle with feta cheese.

5. Bake for 12–14 minutes, or until the tomato mixture is hot and bubbly and the fish flakes with a fork.

6. Serve over pasta. Garnish with parsley.

Citrus Grove Orange Roughy

Serves 2

1/3	cup orange juice or blended citrus juice
2	4 to 6-ounce tilapia, orange roughy, or flounder fillets
1	small lime, lemon, or orange, thinly sliced (6–8 slices)
1–2	tablespoons unsalted butter, melted
1/2	teaspoon lemon pepper
	hot cooked rice pilaf
	chopped fresh parsley or cilantro (for garnish)

1. Preheat oven to 400 degrees.

2. Pour orange juice into a small, shallow baking dish. Place 4 citrus slices in baking dish. Place fish fillets on top of citrus slices.

3. Drizzle fillets with melted butter. Sprinkle with lemon pepper. Place another citrus slice on top of each fish fillet.

4. Bake 12–14 minutes, or until fish flakes easily with a fork.

5. Serve with rice. Garnish with parsley and any remaining citrus slices.

Fish Dijon

Serves 2

2	4–6-ounce tilapia, orange roughy, or flounder fillets
1	tablespoon lemon juice
1/3	cup mayonnaise
2	tablespoons grated Parmesan cheese
2	tablespoons Dijon or Creole mustard
	dash of hot pepper sauce, such as *Tabasco*

1. Preheat oven to 400 degrees.

2. Spray a small broiler pan with nonstick cooking spray. Place fish fillets on pan. Sprinkle with lemon juice. Bake fish for 9 minutes.

3. While fish is baking, combine mayonnaise, Parmesan cheese, mustard, and pepper sauce. Set aside.

4. Remove baked fish fillets from oven. Set oven control to broil. Spread mayonnaise mixture over fish fillets.

5. Broil fish 2–3 minutes, or just until topping turns golden brown and bubbly, and fish flakes easily with a fork.

Fiesta Chicken and Lime Soup

A fiesta is a celebration, and this recipe is a celebration of flavors. It makes more than 2 servings—and you'll be glad it does! Not only will you want seconds, you'll want to have extra to take to work for lunch the next day.

The ingredient list may look long, but this soup can be made and ready to serve in fewer than 30 minutes.

Yield: 6 cups

1	tablespoon vegetable oil
1/2	cup onion, chopped
1	clove garlic, minced
1	16-ounce can navy beans, rinsed and drained
1	15 ½-ounce can hominy, rinsed and drained
1	10-ounce can diced tomatoes and green chilies, undrained
1	cup corn kernels, frozen or canned
2 ½	cups chicken broth
2	teaspoons ground cumin
1	cup coarsely chopped or shredded cooked chicken
1/4	cup crushed tortilla chips
	juice of 1 lime

Accompaniments:

1 cup shredded Monterey Jack or cheddar cheese

1–2 limes, cut into wedges

tortilla chips

1. In a medium saucepan, heat canola oil. Add onion and garlic. Cook and stir just until onion is translucent, 3 to 4 minutes.

2. Add beans, hominy, tomatoes and green chilies, corn, chicken broth, and cumin. Heat until hot.

3. Add chicken, crushed tortilla chips, and lime juice. Simmer about 10 minutes to blend flavors.

4. Ladle hot soup into bowls. Serve with shredded cheese, lime wedges, and tortilla chips.

Cook's notes:

If soup becomes too thick upon reheating, just add additional chicken broth.

Use leftover deli-roasted or grilled chicken in this recipe.

Variations:

Substitute chopped, cooked pork chop for the cooked chicken.

Instead of grating the cheese, cut it into small cubes.

For a little more kick, add a roasted and chopped green chili pepper or a 4-ounce can of chopped green chilies, drained.

Three Cheese and Spinach Lasagna Roll-ups

This recipe takes a few minutes to prepare and assemble, but it takes only 5 minutes to cook. You'll enjoy these vegetable lasagna rolls so much, I'm sure you'll find yourself doubling the recipe sometime for company.

Serves 2

4	lasagna noodles
1	tablespoon olive oil
1/2	cup onion, finely chopped
1	large clove garlic, minced
3	ounces fresh baby spinach (half of a 6-ounce bag)
1/3	cup shredded fresh carrots
1/2	teaspoon dried Italian herb seasoning
1/4	teaspoon crushed red pepper flakes
3/4	cup part-skim ricotta cheese
1/2	cup shredded mozzarella cheese
1/4	cup Parmesan cheese
1	cup tomato-based pasta sauce

1. Cook noodles according to package directions. Rinse with cool water. Drain and set aside until ready for step 4.

2. In a medium skillet, heat oil over medium-high heat. Add onion and garlic. Cook, stirring, just until the onion is translucent. Add spinach, shredded carrots, Italian herb seasoning, and red pepper. Continue stirring until the spinach wilts and carrots are crisp-tender. Set aside to cool slightly.

3. In a medium mixing bowl, combine ricotta, mozzarella, and Parmesan cheeses. Stir in cooled spinach mixture.

4. Place noodles on cutting board. Pat dry with paper towel. Top each noodle with about 1/3 cup of cheese mixture. Spread evenly. Roll up each filled noodle into a spiral.

5. Spread 1 tablespoon of the pasta sauce in the bottom of a shallow baking dish (such as an 8- or 9-inch glass pie plate). Place lasagna roll-ups seam side down on top of the sauce. Spoon 1/4 of the pasta sauce over each lasagna roll-up.

6. Cover, and microwave on high power for 2–3 minutes, or until heated through.

Cook's note:

Ready-to-use shredded carrots are available in the produce section of many supermarkets. If you use these, coarsely chop the carrot shreds before measuring.

Variations:

Substitute 1 cup small curd cottage cheese, drained and squeezed dry in a paper towel for the ricotta cheese.

Use fresh arugula instead of spinach, or use some of each.

Cook 8–10 jumbo pasta shells instead of lasagna noodles. Spoon cheese mixture into the cooked shells. Follow directions above for covering with pasta sauce and heating in the microwave.

If you have fresh basil available, finely chop about 1/4 cup, and add it to the spinach mixture.

Roasting Poultry

There are some important points to remember when roasting poultry.

❋ For dark meat, heat to an internal temperature of 180 degrees. For white meat—an internal temperature of 170 degrees.

❋ It is almost impossible to judge the degree of doneness without an instant-read thermometer. Insert thermometer into the thickest point of poultry—but do not touch the bone.

❋ The breast will be somewhat hard and dry when cooked to temperatures in excess of 170 degrees. When cooking both white and dark meat in the same recipe, the moisture of the white meat can be retained if cooked with the skin intact.

Chicken Roasted
with Tomatoes, Potatoes, and Olives

Nothing smells homier than a chicken roasting in the oven. The addition of olives gives this dish a different flavor twist from the ordinary roasted bird.

Serves 2

1	whole chicken breast with bone, halved
1	pound red potatoes
4	plum tomatoes
8	Kalamata olives, pitted
10	cloves garlic
4	teaspoon fresh lemon juice
5	tablespoons extra virgin olive oil
1	large lemon, sliced thin
1	tablespoon fresh rosemary leaves, chopped
	salt and freshly ground black pepper

1. Preheat oven to 375 degrees.
2. Mash 4 garlic cloves with a small amount of salt to form a paste.
3. In a small bowl, whisk together 4 teaspoons of lemon juice with olive oil, and season with salt and pepper. Add garlic paste, and stir to combine.
4. In a lightly oiled, shallow roasting pan, make two beds by overlapping lemon slices. Place a chicken breast half skin-side up on each bed of lemons.
5. Brush chicken with some of the garlic-lemon mixture, and season with salt and pepper.
6. Quarter potatoes and tomatoes.
7. Arrange vegetables, along with remaining garlic cloves and olives, around chicken breast.
8. Sprinkle rosemary over vegetables and chicken. Drizzle remaining garlic and lemon mixture over vegetables.
9. Using a spoon, gently toss vegetables so all are covered.
10. Roast chicken and vegetables about 35 minutes, or until instant-read thermometer reads 170 degrees.
11. Discard lemon slices, and serve chicken with vegetables. Spoon pan juices over chicken and vegetables.

Cook's notes:

It is best to use fresh rosemary, but dried is okay. Use only 1 teaspoon if using dried.

You can easily double the amount of chicken.

Crab Cakes

You don't have to visit Chesapeake Bay to enjoy delicious crab cakes. This recipe takes you right to the shores with its perfectly seasoned crabmeat and crispy, crunchy exterior.

Yield: 4

2	tablespoons finely chopped shallots
1	large egg, slightly beaten
2	tablespoons mayonnaise
2	tablespoons lemon-pepper bread crumbs (can use seasoned or plain bread crumbs)
1/2	teaspoon *Old Bay* seafood seasoning
1/2	teaspoon dry ground mustard
1/2	teaspoon *Worcestershire* sauce
1/4	teaspoon *Tabasco*
1/4	teaspoon salt
1/8	teaspoon freshly ground black pepper (if not using lemon-pepper bread crumbs)
6	ounces fresh or canned crabmeat, drained, with cartilage removed
	panko (Japanese bread crumbs) for dredging

1. In a mixing bowl, combine the egg and mayonnaise. Add the shallots, bread crumbs, *Old Bay* seasoning, mustard, *Worcestershire* sauce, *Tabasco*, and salt. Fold in crab. Shape into 4 cakes. Refrigerate for 20 minutes.

2. Pour Panko bread crumbs into a small dish. Dredge each crab cake in the bread crumbs, covering all sides.

3. In a medium skillet, cook crab cakes in 2 tablespoons of canola oil on medium heat for 3–5 minutes on each side, or until golden brown. Serve with tartar sauce or dill sauce.

Cook's note:

Panko bread crumbs can be found in the supermarket aisle where the Asian food is found, or near the regular bread crumbs.

Dill Sauce

Yield: 3/4 cup

1/2	cup mayonnaise
1/4	cup sour cream
1–2	tablespoons lemon juice
1/2	tablespoon fresh dill, chopped (add more dill if you like a stronger dill flavor)

1. Combine mayonnaise, sour cream, and lemon juice in a small bowl.
2. Stir in fresh, chopped dill.

Tartar Sauce

Yield: 1/4 cup

1/4	cup mayonnaise
2	tablespoons sweet pickle relish
1	teaspoon lemon juice

Combine mayonnaise, relish, and lemon juice in a small bowl. Mix. Chill until ready to serve.

Cook's notes:

Use real mayonnaise, not salad dressing.

Use the sauces on grilled, broiled, or baked fish.

You can use lowfat mayonnaise and sour cream.

Desserts

Chocolate Brownies

Peanut Butter and Chocolate Martini

Sun-Kissed Lemon Bars

Cherry Crisp

Chocolate Cake

Chocolate Brownies

If you are a chocolate lover, this recipe is sure to please. Any leftovers should be wrapped in plastic wrap. These brownies would make a great addition to any brown-bag lunch.

Serves 6–8

1	square (1 ounce) unsweetened chocolate
2	tablespoons unsalted butter
1	large egg
1/2	cup sugar
1/2	teaspoon vanilla extract
1/3	cup all-purpose flour
1/4	teaspoon baking powder
1/8	teaspoon salt
1/4	cup chopped walnuts or pecans
1/4	cup chocolate or mint-flavored chips

1. Preheat oven to 350 degrees.

2. In a small, heavy saucepan, melt unsweetened chocolate and butter over low heat, stirring constantly until smooth.

3. In a small mixing bowl, stir to combine egg and sugar. Stir in the chocolate mixture and the vanilla.

4. In a mixing bowl, combine the flour, baking powder, and salt. Gradually add the chocolate mixture as you stir.

5. Stir in nuts and chips.

6. Spread into a greased (or lined with foil) 8x4x2-inch loaf pan. If using foil, do not grease the pan, and make sure foil extends over sides for easy removal.

7. Bake for 15–18 minutes, or until toothpick inserted in the middle comes out almost clean. Cool on a wire rack.

Cook's notes:

You may use a disposable aluminum loaf pan—found in the baking section of the supermarket.

*For testing purposes, **Ghirardelli** chocolate was used in this recipe.*

Peanut Butter and Chocolate Martini

This makes a delicious dessert drink when having another couple over for dinner. Special occasion or not, whip up this decadent dessert drink and enjoy.

Serves 2–3

2	cups vanilla ice cream
3	ounces vodka
3	ounces chocolate liqueur (such as *Godiva*)
2	teaspoons creamy peanut butter
	sugar or grated chocolate for around the rim of the martini glass

1. In a blender, combine ice cream, vodka, chocolate liqueur, and peanut butter. Process until smooth and creamy.

2. Dip the rims of martini glasses in chocolate liqueur or water, then into grated chocolate or sugar. Garnish the tops with grated chocolate.

Sun-Kissed Lemon Bars

Just the right combination of sweet and tart, these bars make a wonderful finale to any fish entree.

Yield: 8

1/4	cup unsalted butter, softened
2	tablespoons confectioner's sugar
1/2	cup all-purpose flour

Filling

1	large egg
1/2	cup sugar
2	tablespoons lemon juice
1	tablespoon all-purpose flour
1/8	teaspoon baking powder
1/2	teaspoon confectioner's sugar

1. Preheat oven to 325 degrees.

2. In a small mixing bowl, cream butter and confectioner's sugar. Gradually beat in flour.

2. Line an 8x4x2-inch loaf pan with foil. Press mixture into the bottom of the lined pan.

3. Bake for 14–16 minutes or until set and the edges are lightly browned.

4. For filling, in a mixing bowl, beat the egg, sugar, lemon juice, flour, and baking powder until frothy. Pour over warm crust. Bake for 18–22 minutes, or until lightly browned. Cool on a wire rack. Dust with confectioner's sugar. Cut into bars.

Cherry Crisp

On a cold, winter night there is nothing better than a warm fruit crisp right out of the oven.

Serves 2

Filling

2	cups frozen cherries
2	tablespoons sugar
2	teaspoons cornstarch
1/8	teaspoon almond extract

Topping

1/4	cup sugar
1/4	teaspoon cinnamon
1/4	cup old-fashioned oats
2	tablespoons all-purpose flour
2	tablespoons butter, cut into small pieces

1. Preheat oven to 375 degrees.

2. In a round 2 ½- or 3-cup baking dish, mix all fruit-filling ingredients.

3. In a small bowl, mix all topping ingredients with a fork until crumbly. Sprinkle evenly over fruit mixture.

4. Bake 35–45 minutes, or until topping is light golden brown and fruit is bubbly. Cool 10–15 minutes before eating.

Variation:

Try using frozen blueberries (instead of cherries) with 1/8 teaspoon grated lemon rind.

Chocolate Cake

This chocolate cake is a scaled-down version of my grandmother's very moist chocolate cake recipe. It was always a treat to walk in her back door and see this cake waiting for us on her kitchen counter.

Serves 9

1	cup boiling water
1/4	cup unsalted butter
1	large egg
1	teaspoon vanilla extract
1	cup all-purpose flour
1	cup sugar
3	tablespoons baking cocoa
1	teaspoon baking powder
1/2	teaspoon baking soda
1/4	teaspoon cinnamon
1/4	teaspoon salt
	confectioner's sugar

1. Preheat oven to 350 degrees.

2. In a bowl, combine the flour, sugar, cocoa, baking powder, baking soda, cinnamon, and salt. Set aside.

3. In a mixing bowl, using a handheld electric mixer, beat water and butter until butter is melted. Beat in egg and vanilla.

4. Add flour mixture to the egg mixture, and beat for 2 minutes.

5. Pour into a greased 8x8-inch square baking pan.

6. Bake 25–30 minutes, or until wooden toothpick inserted near the center comes out clean. Cool on a wire rack. Dust with confectioner's sugar.

Cook's notes:

Pieces of cake can be wrapped individually and frozen for a quick dessert later.

The cake is also delicious with a scoop of vanilla ice cream and chocolate syrup drizzled on top.

Appendix

Common Equivalents

Liquid Equivalents

1 cup = 8 fluid ounces or 16 tablespoons

2 cups = 1 pint or 16 fluid ounces

2 pints = 1 quart or 32 fluid ounces

4 quarts = 1 gallon

1/2 tablespoon = 1 ½ teaspoons

1 tablespoon = 3 teaspoons

2 tablespoons = 1 fluid ounce

Dry Equivalents

1/4 cup = 4 tablespoons

1/3 cup = 5 tablespoons plus 1 teaspoon

1/2 cup = 8 tablespoons or roughly 4 ounces

3/4 cup = 12 tablespoons

1 cup = 16 tablespoons

1 dry pint = 2 cups or 1/2 dry quart

1 dry quart = 4 cups or 2 dry pints

1 pound = 16 ounces

Common Equivalents

Food Equivalents

1 slice bread = 1/3 cup fresh bread crumbs

1 stick butter = 8 tablespoons, 1/2 cup, or 4 ounces butter

1 pound butter = 4 sticks butter

1 pound confectioner's sugar = about 4 ½ cups confectioner's sugar, sifted

1 pound granulated sugar = 2 cups granulated sugar

1/2 pound hard cheese = about 2 cups grated cheese

1 cup heavy cream = 2 cups whipped cream

Equivalent Measures and Weights

Dash = less than 1/8 teaspoon

3 teaspoons = 1 tablespoon

2 tablespoons = 1/8 cup or 1 fluid ounce

4 tablespoons = 1/4 cup or 2 fluid ounces

8 tablespoons = 1/2 cup or 4 fluid ounces

12 tablespoons = 3/4 cup or 6 fluid ounces

16 tablespoons = 1 cup or 8 fluid ounces

1 cup = 8 fluid ounces

2 cups = 1 pint or 16 fluid ounces

4 cups = 1 quart

2 pints = 1 quart or 32 fluid ounces

4 quarts = 1 gallon

16 ounces = 1 pound

1 ounce = 28.35 grams

1 liter = 1.06 quarts

Pan Size and Volume

Pan Size	Approximate Volume
2½x1½-inch muffin pan cup	1/2 cup
8½x4½x2½-inch loaf pan	6 cups
9x5x3-inch loaf pan	8 cups
8x8x1½-inch baking pan	6 cups
9x9x1½-inch baking pan	8 cups
9x1-inch pie plate	4 cups
11x7x1½-inch baking pan	8 cups
13x9x2-inch baking pan	15 cups
15½x10½x1-inch jelly roll pan	16 cups

Seasoning and Spice Substitutions

If a recipe calls for:	You may use:
1 teaspoon dried herbs	1 tablespoon fresh herbs
1 teaspoon allspice	1 teaspoon equal parts cinnamon, clove, and nutmeg
1 teaspoon basil	1 teaspoon oregano
1 teaspoon caraway	1 teaspoon anise
1 teaspoon cayenne	1 teaspoon crushed red pepper
1 teaspoon chervil	1 teaspoon parsley or tarragon
1/8 teaspoon garlic powder	1 small garlic clove
1 tablespoon prepared mustard	1 teaspoon dry mustard
1 teaspoon nutmeg	1 teaspoon mace (mace is the outer layer of the whole nutmeg)
1 tablespoon dehydrated, minced onion	1/2 small, fresh onion
1 teaspoon oregano	1 teaspoon marjoram
1 teaspoon sage	1 teaspoon thyme

Average Yields

Apple	1 medium = 1 cup chopped
Apples	3 medium = 3 cups sliced
Bacon	8 slices = 1/2 cup crumbled
Bananas	2 small = 1 medium or 1 cup sliced
Beans, green	1 pound = 3 cups of 1-inch pieces
Butter	1 stick = 4 ounces, 8 tablespoons, 1/2 cup
Blue cheese	1/4 lb = 1 cup crumbled
Broccoli	1 pound = 3 cups florets
Carrots	2 medium = 1 cup 1/4-inch rounds
	1 ½ medium = 1 cup shredded
Cauliflower	1 pound = 3 cups florets
Celery	2 medium stalks = 1 cup 1/4-inch slices
Cheese	4 ounces = 1 cup shredded
	1 pound = 4 cups shredded
Chicken, cooked	2 ½ – 3 pounds = 2 ½ cups diced meat
Corn	2 medium ears = 1 cup kernels
Crumbs, chocolate cookie	19 cookies = 1 cup crushed

Average Yields

Crumbs, graham cracker	16 squares = 1 ¼ cup crushed
Crumbs, saltine	28 squares = 1 cup crushed
Crumbs, vanilla wafer	22 wafers = 1 cup crushed
Eggs	1 large = 1/4 cup or 2 ounces
Egg whites	8–10 = 1 cup
Egg yolks	16 = 1 cup
Garlic	1 medium clove = 1 teaspoon finely chopped
Green pepper	1 medium = 1 cup chopped
Lemon	1 medium = 2 tablespoons juice
Lemon peel	1 = 1 ½–3 teaspoons grated
Macaroni noodles, shells, elbows, etc.	1 pound dry = 9 cups cooked
Mushrooms	8 ounces = 3 cups 1/4-inch slices
Olives	15 large = 1 cup chopped
Onions, green	9 = 1 cup sliced
Onions, white	1 medium = 1–1 ½ cups chopped
Orange	1 = 1/3–1/2 cup juice

Average Yields

Orange peel	1 = 1–2 tablespoons grated
Potatoes	1 medium = 2 cups roughly diced
Raisins	15 ounces = 2 ¾ cups
Rice, brown (raw)	1 cup = 4 cups cooked
Rice, parboiled or converted	1 cup = 2–3 cups cooked
Rice, instant	1 cup = 2 cups cooked
Rice, white regular (raw)	1 cup = 3 cups cooked
Rice, wild (raw)	1 cup = 3 cups cooked
Shrimp	1 ½ pounds raw (in shell), 2 cups cooked
Spaghetti noodles	1 pound dry = 7 cups cooked
Spinach	1 pound fresh leaves = 10–12 cups torn pieces
Tomato	1 medium-large = 1 cup chopped
Plum tomatoes	8 = 1 pound
Strawberry	1 quart = 4 cups sliced
Sugar, brown	1 pound = 2 ¼ cups packed

Glossary of Food Terms

Al dente

Italian for "to the tooth." Describes perfectly cooked pasta—just tender, with slight resistance.

Au gratin

A dish browned in the oven or broiler, usually topped with cheese, bread crumbs, or other crushed ingredients.

Au jus

A French term applied to meat served with only the natural, unthickened pan juices obtained during preparation.

Baste

To spoon or brush a liquid over food to keep it moist during cooking. The liquid can be sauce, marinade, broth, melted butter, or pan juices.

Beat

To briskly mix or stir a mixture with a spoon, whisk, fork, or electric mixer.

Béchamel

A basic white sauce of flour and butter to which milk and seasonings have been added.

Bind

To thicken or smooth the consistency of a liquid, usually using egg yolks, flour, potatoes, or rice.

Bisque

A thick, creamy soup, usually made from fish or vegetable purées.

Blanch

To cook food (usually fruits or vegetables) by briefly dipping into boiling water, then plunging into ice water to stop the cooking. This technique locks in the color, texture, and flavor. Blanching is used to loosen tomato and peach skins (for peeling) and to mellow the saltiness or bitterness of certain foods.

Blend

To mix ingredients until smooth or combined.

Boil

To heat liquid until bubbles break vigorously on the surface. Water boils at 212 degrees. The term also means to cook food, such as pasta, or potatoes, in a boiling liquid.

Braise

To cook food by first browning in fat; then, continuing to cook in a small amount of liquid, on top of stove or in the oven. This slow method tenderizes tough cuts of meat by breaking down their fibers as it develops their flavors.

Broth

A thin, clear liquid produced by simmering vegetables, poultry, meat, or fish (on the bone) in water. Broth is used as a base for soups, stews, sauces, and many other dishes.

Brown

To cook over high heat, usually on top of the stove.

Butterfly

To split food, such as shrimp or boneless leg of lamb, horizontally, cutting almost all the way through, and then opening it up (like a book) to form a butterfly shape. It exposes a more uniform surface area so food cooks evenly and quickly.

Caramelize

To heat sugar until it becomes syrupy and golden-to-deep amber in color. Sugar-topped desserts like crème brûlée are caramelized under the broiler or with a propane torch. Onions become caramelized when slowly cooked until golden brown and very tender.

Core

To remove the seeds or tough woody centers from fruits such as apples, pears, or pineapple, and vegetables such as cabbage and fennel.

Cream

To beat butter, margarine, or other fat (sometimes with sugar) until it's creamy looking, fluffy, and light. This technique beats in air, creating light-textured baked goods.

Crimp

To decoratively pinch or press the dough edges of a single piecrust or to seal the dough edges of a double-crusted pie so the filling doesn't seep out during baking.

Curdle

To coagulate or separate into solids and liquids. Egg- and milk-based mixtures can curdle if heated too quickly, if overcooked, or if combined with an acid such as lemon juice.

Deglaze

To scrape up the flavorful browned bits from the bottom of the skillet or roasting pan. The bits are from meat or poultry that has been cooked by adding water, wine, or broth, and stirred while gently heated.

Devein

To remove the dark intestinal vein of shrimp. The shrimp is first peeled, then a lengthwise slit is made along the back, and the vein is removed.

Dollop

A spoonful of soft food, such as whipped cream.

Dot

To scatter bits of butter or margarine over a pie filling, casserole, or other dish before baking—it adds richness and flavor and helps promote browning.

Dredge

To lightly coat with flour, cornmeal, or bread crumbs. Meats and fish are dredged before cooking to create a deliciously crisp, browned exterior.

Drizzle

To pour, in a fine stream, melted butter, oil, syrup, melted chocolate, or other liquid back and forth over food.

Dust

To coat lightly with confectioner's sugar, cocoa (cakes and pastries), or another powdery ingredient.

Emulsify

To bind liquids that usually can't blend easily, such as oil and vinegar. The trick is to slowly add liquid, usually the oil, to the other ingredients, while mixing vigorously. Natural emulsifiers, such as egg yolks or mustard, are often added to vinaigrettes or sauces to emulsify them for a longer period.

Fond

The concentrated juices, drippings, and bits of food left in pans after foods are roasted or sautéed. It is used to flavor sauces made directly in pans in which the foods are cooked.

Flour

To coat food, a surface, or a baking pan with a light dusting of flour.

Fold

To combine a light mixture (such as beaten egg whites, whipped cream, or sifted flour) with a heavier mixture (such as a cake batter or the base of a soufflé) without deflating either. A rubber spatula is the best tool.

Glaze

To coat food by brushing with melted jelly, jam, or barbecue sauce, or to brush piecrust with milk or beaten egg before baking.

Grill

To cook food directly or indirectly over a source of heat (usually charcoal briquettes, gas, or a special ridged pan). Also, the name of the appliance used for grilling.

Julienne

To cut food, especially vegetables, into thin, uniform, matchstick-shaped strips about 2 inches long.

Knead

To work dough until it is smooth and elastic, either by pressing and folding with the heel of the hand or in a heavy-duty mixer with a dough hook. Kneading develops the flour's gluten, an elastic protein that gives yeast breads their structure.

Leavening

An agent that causes dough or batter to rise. Common leaveners include baking powder, baking soda, and yeast. Natural leaveners are air (when beaten into eggs) and steam (in popovers and cream puffs).

Marinate

To flavor and/or tenderize a food by letting it sit in a liquid (such as lemon juice, wine, yogurt, or oil). When a marinade contains an acid, be sure to marinate in a nonreactive container (glass or plastic). Note: acid from marinade can eat away at cast iron or aluminum, making the food unsafe to eat—never cook spaghetti sauce in a cast-iron pot!

Mustard, Dijon

This prepared mustard gets its distinctive flavor from a special blend of mustard seeds and white wine. There are many different brands with varying heat levels, so when you find a brand you like, stick with it.

Pancetta

An unsmoked bacon that is rolled into a cylinder and sliced to order. It is used in Italian dishes. Pancetta is available at Italian delicatessens, specialty food stores, and some supermarkets. Substitute regular smoked bacon, if necessary.

Old Bay seasoning

An aromatic, somewhat hot blend of ground spices, popular with cooks in the Chesapeake Bay area; especially good for seafood dishes.

Pan fry

To cook food in a small amount of fat in a skillet until browned and cooked through.

Parboil

To partially cook food in boiling water. Carrots are often parboiled before they're added to other foods that take less time to cook.

Pepper

The world's most popular spice. Peppercorns are the dried berries of a perennial vine. They come in four colors: black, white, pink, and green. Freshly ground pepper has an incomparable flavor, so it's worth the investment to purchase a good-quality pepper grinder. Some recipes call for coarse-cracked pepper (also called butcher's grind), but it's just as easy to grind your own peppercorns in a mortar and pestle or with a heavy skillet on a work surface.

Pinch

The amount of a powdery ingredient, such as salt, pepper, or spice, that you can hold between your thumb and forefinger—about 1/16 of a teaspoon.

Poach

To cook food in a gently simmering liquid. The surface should barely move. The amount and type of liquid will depend on the food being poached.

Pound

To flatten to a uniform thickness using a meat mallet, meat pounder, or rolling pin. Meat and poultry is pounded to ensure even cooking. Pounding also tenderizes tough meats by breaking up hard-to-chew connective tissue.

Preheat

To bring an oven or broiler to the desired temperature before cooking food.

Prick

To pierce a food, usually with a fork, to prevent it from puffing up or bursting during cooking/baking.

Proof

To dissolve yeast in a measured amount of warm water (105 degrees to 115 degrees), sometimes with a small amount of sugar, until it becomes foamy.

Prosciutto

A cured, aged, air-dried ham with a firm texture and deliciously salty flavor. Imported Italian prosciutto, available at high-quality grocers and butchers, has a milder flavor than the domestic variety.

Punch down

To deflate yeast dough after it has risen fully. It is not necessary to literally "punch" down the dough. It only needs to be gently deflated.

Purée

To mash or grind food until completely smooth, usually in a food processor, blender, sieve, or food mill.

Reduce

To rapidly boil a liquid, such as sauce, wine, or stock, until it has reduced and the flavor is concentrated.

Render

To slowly cook animal fat or skin until fat separates from its connective tissue. The liquid is strained before being used. The crisp brown bits left in the pan are called crackling.

Roast

To cook, in an uncovered pan in the oven, with dry heat. Roasted food develops a well-browned exterior. Meats and poultry are suitable for roasting, as are many vegetables.

Rolling boil

A full boil that cannot be stirred down.

Salt

There are many kinds of salt available; salt is used primarily for seasoning foods.

Sauté

To cook food quickly in a small amount of hot fat in a skillet. The term derives from the French word *sauter*.

Scald

To heat liquid, such as cream or milk, just until tiny bubbles appear around the edge of pan.

Score

To make shallow cuts (usually parallel or crisscross) in the surface of food before cooking. This is done mainly to facilitate flavor absorption, as in marinated meats, chicken, and fish, but sometimes also for decorative purposes on hams. The tops of breads are often scored to enable them to rise (during baking) without bursting.

Sear

To brown meat, fish, or poultry quickly by placing over very high heat.

Sesame oil

Dark brown-orange in color, this oil is pressed from roasted sesame seeds. It is generally used as a seasoning (not cooking) oil.

Shred

To cut, tear, or grate food items into narrow strips.

Shave

To cut wide, paper-thin slices of food, especially Parmesan cheese or chocolate.

Shuck

To remove the shells of oysters, mussels, scallops, or clams.

Sift

To press ingredients, such as flour or confectioner's sugar, through a sifter or sieve. Sifting incorporates air and removes lumps, which helps ingredients combine more easily.

Simmer

A moist-heat method for cooking food in a liquid over low heat (at about 185 degrees). A few small bubbles should be visible on the surface.

Skim

To remove fat or froth from the surface of a liquid, such as broth, boiling jelly, or soup. A skimmer, a long-handled metal utensil with a flat mesh disk or perforated bowl at one end, is the ideal tool for the job.

Soft peaks

When cream or eggs whites are beaten until they stand in peaks that bend over at the top.

Soy sauce

Made from fermented soybeans and roasted wheat or barley. This dark, salty sauce is indispensable in Asian cooking. There are many different versions, and some can be quite salty. Use a reliable Japanese brand.

Steam

To cook food, covered, over a small amount of boiling water. The food is usually set on a rack or in a basket. Since it's not immersed in water, the food retains more nutrients, color, and flavor than when cooked using other methods.

Stiff peaks

When cream or egg whites are beaten until they stand in firm peaks that hold their shape.

Stir-fry

To cook pieces of food quickly in a small amount of oil over high heat. You stir and toss almost constantly. Stir-frying is used in Asian cooking; a wok is the traditional pan, although a large skillet will do just as well.

Tapenade

A French olive paste seasoned with anchovies, herbs, and garlic. The Italian version is called olivada.

Tahini

Sesame seeds ground into a thick paste; always stir to incorporate the oil that rises to the top. Available at natural food stores and most supermarkets.

Tomatoes, dried

Often referred to as "sun-dried" tomatoes but rarely dried in the sun anymore, these intensely flavored, dehydrated tomatoes are processed by more commercial methods. They can be purchased loose-packed or packed with oil in a jar. Loose-packed dried tomatoes should be soaked in boiling water (enough to fully cover the tomatoes) until softened, then drained.

Temper

To warm food gently before adding it to a hot mixture. Tempering prevents the food from separating or curdling.

Tender-crisp (crisp-tender)

The ideal degree of doneness for many vegetables. They're tender, but retain some crunch.

Toast

To brown bread, croutons, whole spices, or nuts in a dry skillet or in the oven. Toasting enhances the flavor of nuts and makes it possible to remove the skin from hazelnuts.

Toss

To lift and drop pieces of food quickly and gently with two utensils, usually to coat them with a sauce (as for pasta) or dressing (as for salad).

Vinegar

Bacterial activity can turn some liquids into vinegar. The word "vinegar" derives from the French phrase *vin aigre*, which means "sour wine." Cider vinegar, made from apple juice, is a popular vinegar. Distilled white vinegar has a strong flavor but is preferred for pickling because it does not darken food. Red and white wines are also made into vinegars. An ancient process that slowly turns the wine sour instead of inoculating it with fast-acting bacteria produces the more expensive vinegars. Tarragon vinegar is white wine vinegar that has been infused with tarragon. Balsamic vinegar is made from semidry Trebbiano grapes, so the resulting vinegar has a sweet note. Most supermarket varieties are tasty, but they aren't true balsamic vinegars, which are aged for years in wood. Malt vinegar, a British favorite, is a mild vinegar made from malted barley.

Whip

To beat an ingredient (especially heavy cream or whipping cream) or mixture rapidly to incorporate air and increase the volume. You can use a whisk, eggbeater, or electric mixer.

Whisk

To beat ingredients (such as heavy cream, whipping cream, eggs, salad dressing, or sauces) with a fork or whisk to mix, blend, or incorporate air.

Zest

To remove the flavorful colored part of citrus skin. Use the fine holes of a grater, a zester, a vegetable peeler, or a *Microplane*, avoiding the bitter white pith that is underneath.

Kitchen Equipment Resource Guide

Bridge Kitchenware

(bridgekitchenware.com)

An excellent source for cookware.

Williams-Sonoma

(williams-sonoma.com)

Sur La Table

(surlatable.com)

www.culinary.net

Recipes, food, and home resources.

www.epicurious.com

Recipe database and other helpful food information.

R R
ML

10/06